M Drugovich

NEW DIRECTIONS FOR INSTITU

MW00745132

Patrick T. Terenzini
The Pennsylvania State University
EDITOR-IN-CHIEF

Ellen Earle Chaffee
North Dakota University System
ASSOCIATE EDITOR

Increasing Graduate Student Retention and Degree Attainment

Leonard L. Baird
University of Kentucky

EDITOR

Number 80, Winter 1993

JOSSEY-BASS PUBLISHERS
San Francisco

INCREASING GRADUATE STUDENT RETENTION
AND DEGREE ATTAINMENT
Leonard L. Baird (ed.)
New Directions for Institutional Research, no. 80
Volume XV, Number 4
Patrick T. Terenzini, Editor-in-Chief
Ellen Earle Chaffee, Associate Editor

Microfilm copies of issues and articles are available in 16mm and 35mm,
as well as microfiche in 105mm, through University Microfilms Inc., 300
North Zeeb Road, Ann Arbor, Michigan 48106-1346.

LC 85-645339   ISSN 0271-0579   ISBN 1-55542-675-1

NEW DIRECTIONS FOR INSTITUTIONAL RESEARCH is part of The Jossey-Bass
Higher and Adult Education Series and is published quarterly by Jossey-
Bass Inc., Publishers, 350 Sansome Street, San Francisco, California
94104-1342. Second-class postage paid at San Francisco, California, and
at additional mailing offices. POSTMASTER: Send address changes to New
Directions for Instiutional Research, Jossey-Bass Inc., Publishers, 350 Sansome Street, San Francisco, California 94104-1342.

SUBSCRIPTIONS for 1993 cost $47.00 for individuals and $62.00 for institutions, agencies, and libraries.

EDITORIAL CORRESPONDENCE should be sent to the Editor-in-Chief, Patrick
T. Terenzini, Center for the Study of Higher Education, The Pennsylvania
State University, 403 South Allen Street, Suite 104, University Park,
Pennsylvania 16801-5202.

Photograph of the library by Michael Graves at San Juan Capistrano by
Chad Slattery © 1984. All rights reserved.

Manufactured in the United States of America. Nearly all Jossey-Bass
books, jackets, and periodicals are printed on recycled paper that contains
at least 50 percent recycled waste, including 10 percent postconsumer
waste. Many of our materials are also printed with vegetable-based inks;
during the printing process, these inks emit fewer volatile organic com-
pounds (VOCs) than petroleum-based inks. VOCs contribute to the for-
mation of smog.

CONTENTS

EDITOR'S NOTES

Whether measured in budget, increases in enrollment, or attention from administrators, graduate education is assuming a larger role at most institutions. Graduate education warrants this attention if only because its highly labor-intensive character makes it the most expensive area of higher education. In addition, graduate education is the training ground for some of the most valued graduates of our universities. That is, society's needs for health professionals, teachers, social workers, researchers, professors, and a variety of technical professionals are met by graduate education. Thus, for reasons of both cost and social importance, the progress of students in graduate education becomes a critical matter. This issue has become even more salient in recent years as evidence has accumulated that the duration of study or time to degree has steadily crept upward. For example, over the last twenty years, the average time from the bachelor's degree to completion of the doctorate has risen from 8.0 years to 10.5 years. Over the same period, registered time has increased from 5.5 to 6.9 years. Although national data are not available for master's programs, studies conducted at individual institutions suggest a similar pattern. Moreover, there is some evidence that degree completion rates have dropped over the same period (Bowen and Rudenstine, 1992).

For these reasons, national, state, and institutional concern about the progress of graduate students has grown in the last few years, and institutional researchers can increasingly expect to be called on to study this area. This volume is intended to help researchers conduct such studies with skill and confidence.

In Chapter One, Leonard Baird discusses the general nature of graduate education, the factors that seem to affect duration and completion, and models of graduate student retention and attrition. Baird stresses the importance of recognizing that the influences on retention in graduate education differ from those in undergraduate education in many but not all respects.

In Chapter Two, Paul Isaac discusses some conceptual and technical details that should be attended to before studies of graduate student progress are undertaken: what it means to seek and obtain a master's degree, when a doctoral student can be considered to have dropped out, and other difficulties that arise from the flexibility of graduate education. Isaac offers practical solutions to these problems, outlines ways to coordinate information about graduate students that is often scattered across the institution, and details the elements needed in a data set for studying graduate student progress.

In Chapter Three, Maresi Nerad and Joseph Cerny describe the experience of the University of California at Berkeley in examining graduate student completion rates and times to degree. Nerad and Cerny outline the step-by-step process used not only to understand but to attempt to improve graduate

1

student progress. Other institutions concerned about retaining students and speeding their progress to their degrees could make use of this process. (I would like to thank the Council of Graduate Schools for permission to make use of an earlier version of this chapter.)

In Chapter Four, Amaury Nora and Alberto Cabrera describe some advanced statistical approaches to the study of graduate student progress. They show how conceptual and statistical models can be used to examine graduate student retention. Using data from the University of Illinois at Chicago, they focus on the importance of integrating graduate students into the department.

In Chapter Five, James Ploskonka shows how institutional researchers can use a readily available existing data set to examine doctoral-level education at their institution. The National Research Council obtains considerable data from each recipient of the Ph.D., and these data are available to institutions in tape form. Ploskonka shows how these data can be used to study patterns of time to degree and differences associated with field, gender, age, sources of finances, and parental education. He also demonstrates how the data can be used in different kinds of analyses of time to degree.

In Chapter Six, Susan Lipschutz discusses the positive role that administrators can play in helping graduate departments to identify and overcome impediments to students' progress. Lipschutz also discusses the active force that administration, especially the graduate school, can be in providing students and departments with cross-disciplinary help.

In Chapter Seven, Leonard Baird provides a guide to the literature on graduate student progress in four areas: general perspectives that can help researchers think about graduate education; analytical techniques that are particularly appropriate to graduate education; specific policy issues, such as minority representation and time to the doctorate; and organizational resources.

In sum, the information in this volume should help those interested in studying and improving graduate student progress—administrators, graduate school staff, departmental chairs, faculty, and institutional researchers—by improving their understanding of graduate education and the ways it can be affected.

Leonard L. Baird
Editor

Reference

Bowen, W. G., and Rudenstine, N. L. *In Pursuit of the Ph.D.* Princeton, N.J.: Princeton University Press, 1992.

LEONARD L. BAIRD is professor and director of the Office of Higher Education Research in the Department of Educational Policy Studies and Evaluation, University of Kentucky, Lexington.

*The implications of current research and theoretical models of gradu-
ate student progress for understanding and studying graduate student
retention and time to degree are examined.*

Using Research and Theoretical
Models of Graduate Student Progress

Leonard L. Baird

Graduate education is a major part of American higher education, with more
than one and a half million students enrolled in graduate programs. Graduate
students represent nearly one out of every four students attending universities
or comprehensive institutions. Looked at in another way, about one in four
college graduates enters postgraduate study. Thus, graduate education deserves
study if only because of the large number of students involved. However, it
also deserves study because it is the path to many critically important positions
in our society since its programs form researchers, health professionals, teachers, managers, professors, and a great array of technical workers. Moreover,
graduate education is the most costly area of higher education. Because classes
tend to be small and education often involves one-on-one interactions between
professors and students and because the necessary equipment and facilities are
often expensive, the cost per student is high. For all these reasons—the numbers, importance, and costs of graduate education—the retention and progress
of graduate students should be major issues.

What do we know about the retention and progress of graduate students?
First, graduate students differ from undergraduate students in many ways, just
as graduate departments differ from undergraduate colleges. These differences
limit the appropriateness of models of undergraduate retention and progress.
Graduate students are older, they are familiar with higher education and their
own discipline, they usually have experience working, and they often have
many adult and family responsibilities. Although some aspects of undergraduate retention models may apply, especially the Bean and Metzner (1985)
model for nontraditional students, these models would seem to need to be
interpreted in different ways. For example, the financial situations of graduate

students are very different from those of undergraduate students. Second, the definition of *retention* is more problematical for graduate than it is for undergraduate students, as Isaac explains in Chapter Two of this volume. For example, it is not always clear when a student has dropped out or ceased pursuit of the degree that he or she was seeking. Third, graduate education can be very lengthy. In 1991, the average recipient of the doctoral degree required 10.4 years from receipt of his or her bachelor's degree, and he or she was registered for seven years. This extended time is costly for both students and institutions. Thus, time to degree is an important issue for graduate education. This volume considers its importance to equal that of retention. This chapter examines current research and theoretical models of graduate student progress for insights that may help our thinking on these issues.

Synthesizing the Studies

Studies of attrition and time to degree in graduate education suggest a number of variables that seem to be important (Baird, 1990a; Berelson, 1960; Bowen and Rudenstine, 1992; Girves and Wemmerus, 1988; Gunn and Sanford, 1988; Tuckman, Coyle, and Bae, 1990; Wilson, 1965). Several of these variables concern decisions made prior to entry: delayed entrance to graduate school (perhaps as a result of other responsibilities or of less intense interest); pursuit of the graduate degree at an institution different from the bachelor's institution (the two institutions may define the field in different ways; the graduate student is not familiar with faculty at the new institution); and change in discipline (the graduate student needs to complete courses and obtain knowledge that students with undergraduate degrees in the field already possess). Some factors in attrition and time to degree involve students' employment situation: full-time work outside the university, assistantships or fellowships inside the department, and full- or part-time attendance. (Attendance status affects the speed with which requirements can be met and hence the likelihood that other responsibilities will become important.) Likewise, both marriage and children tend to create delays or end progress toward the degree, especially for women.

At the departmental level, students appear to make better progress in departments that have coherent and well thought out programs and regular procedures for monitoring students' progress; that use the resources available to fund as many students as possible through a mixture of assistantships, fellowships, grants, and loans; that help students to identify dissertation topics early in their program; and that create ample opportunities for informal interaction among students and between faculty and students. Disciplines clearly differ. Time to degree is shortest in the bench sciences, such as chemistry, and the mathematical disciplines. It is longer in the social sciences and longest in the humanities. The difference in average time to doctorate between the fastest and slowest disciplines is four years (Baird, 1990b). All these factors could be examined in studies of graduate student degree progress at particular institutions. As such, they would be studied in isolation. However, they can also be considered as part of the several models of graduate student progress discussed in the next section.

Research Models of Graduate Student Progress

Graduate education has been described as a process of socialization to an ultimate professional role (Baird, 1990a; Stein and Weidman, 1990). This process involves learning the "specialized knowledge, skills, attitudes, values, norms, and interests of the profession" (Bragg, 1976, p. 1). The graduate faculty is the critical agent conducting this socialization, since its members define knowledge and disciplinary values, model the roles of academics in the discipline, and produce practical help and advice (Stein and Weidman, 1990). Graduate student peers are the other socialization agent (Baird, 1990a; Tinto, 1991); this group is seldom given formal recognition. Thus, socialization at the graduate level would appear to involve processes similar to those at the undergraduate level described as academic and social integration (Tinto, 1987, 1991). However, these concepts have a different meaning at the graduate level and vary with the stages of the academic career (Baird, 1972, 1990a; Katz, 1976; Tinto, 1991). That is, as students progress through their program, they become integrated into their institution, department, and discipline. Since the different stages of the graduate career have different tasks and demands, the relations of students with faculty and other students also differ. As students progress through their program, they are increasingly assimilated into the life of the department and discipline, and their access to and interactions with faculty increase as a result (Baird, 1972; Tinto, 1991). Especially among doctoral students, those at the beginning of their program are still learning the expectations and demands that the discipline places on them, and they are thus somewhat distant from faculty. Those at the dissertation stage have served their apprenticeships, have been socialized to the norms and methods of the discipline, and are expected to work closely with faculty. Likewise, students at the beginning of their programs may see other students as unknown quantities or as competitors in contrast to students at later stages, who view other students as part of a departmental community (Lozoff, 1976; Baird, 1990a).

The demands and opportunities of the course work and other program requirements also change over the course of graduate study. In general, the course work and requirements increasingly emphasize the norms and methods of the discipline (Katz, 1976). This emphasis on particular techniques and ideas is at the heart of socialization to the discipline. In general, course work places the emphasis on learning to be an observer, on making independent use of methods that the discipline considers elegant, and on delimiting constructs to fit the approaches that dominate the discipline (Taylor, 1976; Baird, 1990a). However, in the process of focusing on an intellectual approach to knowing that emphasizes objectivity and independence, students need to reject other approaches, usually those that depend on relationships with other people or on unintellectual approaches, such as intuition (Taylor, 1976; Lozoff, 1976; Baird, 1990a).

There have been several attempts to develop models describing the stages of the graduate career. These models have rather different intentions and theoretical perspectives. The results of these examinations also have different implications for studies of retention and time to degree. However, they all tend to fit into the integrated model described later in this section.

A Psychological Model. Katz (1976), whose main interest was the personality development of graduate students, particularly the interaction between intellectual growth and personal development, described the course of graduate students through their studies. Entering students go through a period of insecurity during which their sense of mastery is severely challenged. This sense of inadequacy is enhanced by an idealistic image of the discipline and professors. Students at this stage see themselves as being very far from achieving the ideal. This stage is followed by a period of active coping during which the work is gradually seen as more manageable. Simultaneously, course work, discussions with peers and more advanced students, and interactions with faculty inside and outside class lead to a more realistic view of the demands of the discipline and professors. Gradually, students develop reasonably realistic professional identities. However, Katz emphasizes that mastery of the preferred epistemological and methodological systems of the discipline restricts the student's view of reality. Intense mastery of one area can lead students to confine their thinking to the categories favored by the field of study. Eventually, however, many students also grasp the tentative hypothetical nature of knowledge and the changing multiplicity of reality. This tension between the constraining forms of a discipline and the need for alternative creative views of one's subject is prevalent both in the late years of graduate study and throughout the career of a scholar.

Katz (1976) describes other tensions that characterize the late stages of graduate study. These include the tension between submitting to the authority of the student's professors and the need for autonomy. This tension is sometimes demonstrated in departmental policies. For example, some departments are very flexible in terms of course and experiential requirements, while others construct and enforce very strict rules and regulations. Another important tension pits the ideal of the disinterested and somewhat unworldly scholar against the grant getting, politicking, and pursuit of fashionable topics that is often needed to succeed in academe. Again, students may experience this tension throughout their careers.

In this model, attrition and slow progress are connected in the early period with a strong sense of inadequacy and an overly idealistic view of the discipline and professors; in the middle period with a lack of interactions with other students and faculty; and in the later period with insufficient focusing of interests and in willingness to follow faculty leads.

A Sociologically Oriented Model. Tinto (1991) has also been concerned with understanding the factors in student persistence in doctoral studies. He proposed three general stages: transition to membership in the graduate community, attaining candidacy through the development of competence, and active research. In the first stage, students seek membership in the academic and social communities of the students and faculty in their departments and determine whether the norms and values of those communities are consonant with their own. In the second stage, the emphasis turns to developing recognized competencies. The student's peers and professors use interactions inside and outside the classroom to judge the student's competence. During the last stage, which corresponds to the period in which the student writes the dissertation, the behavior of the major professor assumes paramount importance. For some students, external commitments to family and work become more important at this stage than they were earlier. Aid and assistantships also play a role in persistence, although it is far from simple. In this model, attrition and slow progress are connected in the first stage with low rates of social and academic interactions in the department and low commitment to degree and career goals; in the second stage with inadequate interactions concerning academic competence; and in the last stage with the behavior of a specific faculty member.

A Process Model. Analysis of the ways in which graduate students learn the forms of discourse that prevail within their discipline (Berkenkotter, Huckin, and Ackerman, 1991) leads to a model of the processes rather than the stages of graduate careers. The central task facing entering graduate students is to master new ways of speaking, reading, and writing that are the norm in the disciplinary and departmental community they are entering. As summarized by Berkenkotter, Huckin, and Ackerman (1991, p. 193), the model is based on the following: "(1) Members of a research community share a 'model of knowing.' This model of knowing is embedded in the research methodology that incoming students in graduate programs learn and is encoded in the language that community members use. (2) A research community extends beyond a student's graduate school to include researchers at other institutions. The vanguard of these researchers constitutes an 'invisible college' wherein they share their work with one another through publications in professional journals and through papers delivered at professional meetings. (3) Papers and publications are among a research community's communicative forums: significant issues are raised, defined, and debated within these forums. In this sense, to publish and be cited is to enter the community's discourse. (4) Graduate students are initiated into the research community through the reading and writing they do, through instruction in research methodology, and through interaction with faculty and with their peers. A major part of this initiation process is learning how to use appropriate written linguistic conventions for communicating through disciplinary forums."

These processes of entering the community involve acquiring genre knowledge and joining the conversation among researchers in the field. For example, Swales and Najjar (1987) have analyzed the ways in which researchers write articles based on the anticipated reactions of peer colleagues in their own and other institutions. Students learn to make these anticipations through interactions with faculty as well as by following the models for articles that are available in the literature. Thus, students learn to speak, write, and think like the members of their discipline, as represented initially by their professors and later by other members of the discipline encountered directly in meetings and colloquia and indirectly through journal articles, books, and so forth. Incorporation of these community-defining forms of thinking and discourse into the dissertation and other research efforts plays a vital part in the general process of socialization to the professional role. In this model, attrition and slow time to degree are associated with insufficient comprehension of the "model of knowing" favored by the department, unsatisfactory interactions with professors, and inadequate mastery of the linguistic conventions of the discipline.

An Integrated Model. Although these three conceptions of graduate student socialization are based on different theoretical viewpoints, they all emphasize the importance of several aspects of the graduate experience: faculty—the agents of socialization who define the role to be mastered and the standards of performance to be met—and graduate student peers—the agents who help students develop coping strategies for mastering these definitions and meeting these standards. Both agencies also offer interpersonal support and rewards. Thus, as students move through the program and are more completely socialized, they should become closer to their professors and peers both professionally and personally.

As students master the norms and forums of discourse in their discipline, they are empowered with the skills that their discipline emphasizes and the opportunities to exercise their mastery increase. These changes should be shown in two ways: Students should report increasing opportunities to practice their developing skills in their program experiences, especially in the forms of reasoning that the disciplinary community emphasizes, and they should report gains in their own ability to use these conceptual tools. Simultaneously, following Katz (1976) and Baird (1990a), students should report a narrowing of experiences and little growth in more general intellectual areas.

In addition, it is clear that students often have other roles, including those of spouse or partner, parent, employee, citizen, and so on. These roles can support or subvert students' progress depending on their number, intensity, and—most important—the degree of psychological support that they provide. For example, students with psychologically supportive spouses, employers, and groups may be more likely to stick with their degree plans than students who have fellowships but who do not have the same degree of psychological support. The extent to which these roles further or retard students' graduate student roles directly affects their progress.

In this model, attrition is associated with poor social and academic relationships with professors and fellow students, inadequate mastery of the forms of reasoning favored by the discipline, and poor support from spouses, employers, and other groups. The processes described in these models are clearly affected by students' life conditions. If students do not have time for the sorts of interactions that all the models consider important, they will be less likely to complete their degrees or move ahead on schedule. Thus, students who work outside the university; who have other commitments, such as children; and who cannot afford to pursue full-time study are more likely to drop out or make slow progress. Students who have assistantships, who have few other commitments, and who attend full-time will tend to be successful.

On the departmental side, departments that make an effort to integrate students socially and academically into the community of the department, that are clear about the ways in which students can master the discipline's methods and language by completing a logical sequence of courses and experiences, and that carefully monitor students' progress should have high completion rates and short times to degree.

Using Research and Theoretical Models in Institutional Studies

What would be a reasonable course of action for the institutional researcher who was called upon to study graduate student progress? I would suggest the following actions, which are based on the research and theoretical models just described. They are roughly ordered from the simplest and least costly to the most complex and most costly.

The easiest and quickest action is to obtain the National Research Council tapes of doctoral recipients for the institutional researchers' institution described by Ploskonka in Chapter Five. The most recent ten-year span of data for one's institution should provide sufficient cases for subgroup analyses and the charting of trends. One can compare the time-to-degree figures for discipline, gender, source of financial support, number of dependents, age group, and other variables suggested by research and theory as illustrated by Abedi and Benkin (1987) and by Ploskonka in Chapter Five. These comparisons can be provided very rapidly.

As an alternative, one could use institutional records along the lines outlined by Isaac in Chapter Two. The actual cost and complexity of the effort would depend on the nature of the institution's records. In some institutions, extensive histories of students are readily available in a central file. At others, the data are scattered around the institution, so the task would be to coordinate files. In the worst cases, the institution keeps the records for graduate students in individual folders, so that data for all but the most rudimentary information must be hand-coded by going through voluminous files. Once the data have been assembled, student progress can be assessed by following the procedures described by Isaac in Chapter Two. Again, to understand the processes at work, it may be important to disaggregate the data and conduct separate analyses by discipline, gender, age, and so on.

The third alternative is to survey current graduate students with the strategies followed by Gillingham, Seneca, and Taussig (1991), who asked graduate students to indicate how much time they had spent in pursuit of their degree to date and how much time they believed they would need to complete their degree. By adding these two together, one can estimate total time to degree. In addition, students' intention to leave can be studied by following the example of Metzner and Bean (1987), who asked students Do you expect to return to this school next semester? and Do you expect to return to this school next year? The researchers found that answers to these two questions were major predictors of actual dropout. Similar items could be used in a study of graduate students' intention to leave. Other variables in the survey should include those that other studies have shown to be important: discipline, age, sources of support, marital status, number of dependents, type of employment (off-campus related to studies, off-campus unrelated to studies, on-campus, nonacademic, research assistantship, teaching assistantship), number of hours worked, fellowship status, citizenship, dates of bachelor's degree and start of graduate study, undergraduate discipline, undergraduate institution, undergraduate grades, and graduate grades. Variables suggested by the models described earlier in this chapter include the quality of interactions with faculty and peers; confidence in one's intellectual abilities; stage of academic career; sense of mastery of the research approaches of the discipline; supportiveness of spouse, employer, and other groups; commitment to the discipline; commitment to obtaining the degree; relationships with advisers; and the economic and personal significance of obtaining the degree. Information about departmental practices can be obtained from questions about the clarity and logical sequence of requirements, the extent of attempts to orient new students, whether a master's degree is required for entrance to doctoral studies, the extent to which students' progress is monitored, and the amount of departmental and university red tape. Institutional researchers whose experience in the development of questionnaires is limited can consult texts on questionnaire design and surveying. The volumes by Converse and Presser (1986), who provide counsel on simplicity, clarity, specificity, wording, alternatives, and pretesting, and by Dillman (1978), who provides advice on all stages of mail and telephone surveying, are particularly recommended. Of course, it would be wise to ask groups that have a stake in graduate education, including the graduate school, departmental directors of graduate study, and graduate student associations, to review a draft questionnaire and suggest improvements. Analysis of the resulting data can follow the examples described by the contributors to this volume as well as the resources discussed in the last chapter. The preparation and dissemination of reports can follow the suggestions of Baird (1980).

Fourth in terms of complexity but perhaps not of cost is to follow the procedures outlined by Nerad and Cerny in Chapter Three of this volume. Their procedure has three steps: calculating average times to degree and completion rates for all departments; interviewing graduate students and faculty in departments with long times to degree and low completion rates and in departments with short times to degree and high completion rates; and comparing and contrasting interview findings. The results could help in identifying particular practices and policies that are associated with the observed effects.

Detailed analyses could be done on the factors that were shown to be most important.

The fifth alternative is to begin a longitudinal study of graduate students. Institutional records could be combined with an entrance survey concerning students' backgrounds, initial plans, commitments, and views of their discipline. Retention and progress toward the degree could be studied after one year. Among master's students, degree completion could be studied after two years. Yearly or biennial surveys of students' experiences and views based on the models discussed in this chapter could be conducted to gain an in-depth understanding of the factors involved in retention and time to degree. The details of any such study would need to be worked out, but the eventual outcomes should be specific changes in policies and practices. A longitudinal project currently under way among graduate students at the University of Illinois, Chicago, is designed in this way (Baird and Smart, 1991).

In Chapter Three, Nerad and Cerny suggest some next steps that could be used with the results of any of the actions just described. Meetings and task forces could be organized to consider actions that the institution can take to improve students' progress. From the experiences of educators at Berkeley (reported in Chapter Three) and at Michigan (reported by Lipschutz in Chapter Six), one useful step would be to prepare resource guides that provided departments with ideas for practices and student support services that seem to lead to student progress. Another would be to hold dissertation workshops to help students focus on topics, conduct literature reviews, formulate research questions, gather and analyze data, and—most important—complete the writing of the dissertation.

The key to the utility of any study is the extent to which it affects actual behavior. The kinds of studies discussed here are useful mainly in improving the quality of the decisions that are made, as Lipschutz observes in Chapter Six and Nerad and Cerny point out in Chapter Three. Such studies enable the decision maker to improve his or her understanding of what is happening in graduate education and thereby to understand the consequences of current policies or programs, plan new actions realistically, and anticipate the outcomes of future decisions accurately. The chapters that follow outline some procedures that provide information that bears on decisions that can strengthen graduate education.

References

Abedi, J., and Benkin, E. "The Effects of Students' Academic, Financial, and Demographic Variables on Time to Doctorate." *Research in Higher Education,* 1987, 17, 3–14.

Baird, L. L. "The Relation of Graduate Students' Role Relations to Their Stage of Academic Career, Employment, and Academic Success." *Organizational Behavior and Human Performance,* 1972, 7, 428–441.

Baird, L. L. "Using Campus Surveys for Improving Colleges." In L. L. Baird, R. T. Hartnett, and Associates, *Understanding Student and Faculty Life.* San Francisco: Jossey-Bass, 1980.

Baird, L. L. "The Melancholy of Anatomy: The Personal and Professional Development of

Graduate and Professional School Students." In J. C. Smart (ed.), *Higher Education: Handbook of Theory and Research*. Vol. 6. New York: Agathon Press, 1990a.

Baird, L. L. "Disciplines and Doctorates: The Relationships Between Program Characteristics and the Duration of Doctoral Study." *Research in Higher Education,* 1990b, *31,* 369–385.

Baird, L. L., and Smart, J. C. "The Graduate Student Experience: Theoretical and Research Rationale for a Project to Study Graduate Education." Paper presented at the annual meetings of the Association for the Study of Higher Education, Boston, Oct. 1991.

Bean, J. P., and Metzner, B. S. "A Conceptual Model of Nontraditional Undergraduate Student Attrition." *Review of Educational Research,* 1985, *55,* 485–540.

Berelson, B. *Graduate Education in the United States.* New York: McGraw-Hill, 1960.

Berkenkotter, D., Huckin, T. N., and Ackerman, J. "Social Context and Socially Constructed Texts: The Initiation of a Graduate Student into a Writing Research Community." In C. Bazerman and J. Paradis (eds.), *Textual Dynamics of the Professions: Historical and Contemporary Studies of Writing in Professional Communities.* Madison: University of Wisconsin Press, 1991.

Bowen, H. S., and Rudenstine, N. L. *In Pursuit of the Ph.D.* Princeton, N.J.: Princeton University Press, 1992.

Bragg, A. K. *The Socialization Process in Higher Education.* ERIC/Higher Education Research Report No. 7. Washington, D.C.: American Association for Higher Education, 1976.

Converse, J. M., and Presser, S. *Survey Questions: Handcrafting the Standardized Questionnaire.* Newbury Park, Calif.: Sage, 1986.

Dillman, D. A. *Mail and Telephone Surveys: The Total Design Method.* New York: Wiley, 1978.

Gillingham, L., Seneca, J. J., and Taussig, M. K. "The Determinants of Progress to the Doctoral Degree." *Research in Higher Education,* 1991, *32,* 449–468.

Girves, J. E., and Wemmerus, V. "Developing Models of Graduate Student Degree Progress." *Journal of Higher Education,* 1988, *59,* 163–189.

Gunn, D. S., and Sanford, T. R. "Doctoral Student Retention." *College and University,* 1988, *63,* 374–382.

Katz, J. "Development of the Mind." In J. Katz and R. T. Hartnett (eds.), *Scholars in the Making.* New York: Ballinger, 1976.

Lozoff, M. M. "Interpersonal Relations and Autonomy." In J. Katz and R. T. Hartnett (eds.), *Scholars in the Making.* New York: Ballinger, 1976.

Metzner, B. S., and Bean, J. P. "The Estimation of a Conceptual Model of Nontraditional Undergraduate Student Attrition." *Research in Higher Education,* 1987, *27,* 15–38.

Stein, E., and Weidman, J. "The Socialization of Doctoral Students to Academic Norms." Paper presented at the annual meeting of the American Educational Research Association, Boston, Apr. 1990.

Swales, J., and Najjar, H. "The Writing of Research Articles: Where to Put the Bottom Line?" *Written Communication,* 1987, *4,* 175–191.

Taylor, A. E. "Becoming Observers and Specialists." In J. Katz and R. T. Hartnett (eds.), *Scholars in the Making.* New York: Ballinger, 1976.

Tinto, V. *Leaving College: Rethinking the Causes and Cures of Student Attrition.* Chicago: University of Chicago Press, 1987.

Tinto, V. "Toward a Theory of Doctoral Persistence." Paper presented at the annual meeting of the American Educational Research Association, Chicago, Apr. 1991.

Tuckman, H., Coyle, S., and Bae, Y. *On Time to the Doctorate.* Washington, D.C.: National Academy Press, 1990.

Wilson, K. M. *Of Time and the Doctorate: Report of an Inquiry into the Duration of Doctoral Study.* Atlanta: Southern Regional Education Board, 1965.

LEONARD L. BAIRD *is professor and director of the Office of Higher Education Research in the Department of Educational Policy Studies and Evaluation, University of Kentucky, Lexington.*

The definitions, measures, data, and people needed to study retention of master's and doctoral students are outlined, and practical advice for the institutional researcher is offered.

Measuring Graduate Student Retention

Paul D. Isaac

Information about retention or attrition is notably absent from reports about graduate education. While the literature on undergraduate retention and attrition is fairly extensive, not much has been written about graduate retention. In their comprehensive study of six fields at ten major research universities, Bowen and Rudenstine (1992, p. 107) note that "surprisingly little has been written about the general pattern of completion rates." They report that about half of entering students eventually get a Ph.D., a figure that seems to be in keeping with rules of thumb common among graduate administrators. However, apparently no national data and very little institution-specific data on attrition or retention are available at the graduate level.

Why Do We Not Know Much About Graduate Student Retention?

Undoubtedly, a number of factors account for the apparent lack of attention to attrition, retention, and completion rates for graduate students. Perhaps the most obvious reason is that graduate education is typically less structured and more individualized than undergraduate education, especially for doctoral-level students. Graduate students can more easily avoid registering for a year or more, a practice that slows their progress and complicates attempts to document retention.

Student degree intentions also complicate the assessment of retention of graduate students. Some students enter with plans to complete a master's degree, others plan to obtain only a doctoral degree, still others plan to obtain both, while some have no degree plans. Measures of completion or retention will be affected by how the doctorate-intending student who gets only the master's degree is viewed: Is that a success or a failure? Perhaps more basically, how is the student's degree intent determined? Some applicants indicate that they plan to pursue a doctorate simply to increase their chances of being admitted to a graduate program, even if they actually plan not to continue beyond the master's degree. If a student changes from nondegree to degree status, what is to be the time of admission: original time of first enrollment or time when admitted into the degree program? The choice makes a difference if time cut-offs are to be used in measuring retention.

What about students who change graduate program before they attain a degree? Changes of major are common for undergraduate students. However, a change of major for a graduate student generally means application and admission to a new graduate program. Does this change count as attrition from the first program? What about students who come from another institution with a graduate degree in hand? Does the time spent at the other institution count toward the time spent in the current program? In particular, should the time spent on a master's obtained at another institution count toward the Ph.D. program in the new institution? Although there are no hard-and-fast rules, decisions generally must be made in dealing with these factors, and how one resolves these issues has an important bearing on the results of any study of retention and time to degree.

What Is Meant by Retention?

Retention is often discussed in the context of recruitment (for example, Council of Graduate Schools Task Force, 1990; Middleton and Mason, 1987). Recruitment programs are regarded as doomed to failure if retention programs are not also in place. Recruiting students only to have them drop out before they attain a degree does not generate an atmosphere attractive to prospective students. However, simply keeping students enrolled is not the ultimate goal: They must complete their degree programs. In the discussion that follows, the terms *retention, attrition,* and *degree completion* are used as the context dictates. Our primary concern is about getting students through their degree programs.

We need to be clear about four terms if we are to discuss retention: *entering cohort, attrition, retention,* and *degree completion.*

Entering Cohort. The expression *entering cohort* refers to a group of degree-seeking students who begin their graduate programs at roughly the same time. In some cases, this cohort can be defined as all students who enter in a given year. In other cases, a particular quarter or semester may be of interest. For example, the autumn term is a common reference for public institutions, which receive state funding based on enrollments during this quarter. However, except for special purpose studies, the entering cohort generally includes new students from each of the four quarters (or three semesters) in an academic year. Further, we are usually interested only in the students who enter a degree program, not in students who take graduate courses for personal satisfaction or certification purposes.

We must also decide whether to consider degree intent or completion of previous graduate degrees when we define *cohort*. For example, those who indicate that they are pursuing a master's degree or those who received the master's from another institution may constitute their own cohorts. The safest approach is to collect data on all entering degree-seeking students in a given year and then subdivide them into master's, doctoral, previous degrees, and other categories as appropriate later.

Attrition. *Attrition* generally refers to the failure of a student who has been enrolled to continue her or his studies; that is, the student has dropped out of the program. The nature of graduate education complicates the assessment of attrition because students who are viewed as being in good standing by their graduate program may not actually enroll in a given year. For example, they may not enroll because they are on an internship that is part of the expectations of the program. Or they may take a full-time job prior to completion of the doctoral degree but continue working on the doctoral dissertation while not enrolled. Other students may leave graduate studies for a time and then return to complete the degree program. Still others may pursue graduate studies part-time, which can result in irregular enrollment patterns. Some programs and institutions permit absences of several years without penalty, while others require continuous enrollment following the doctoral general examination.

These complications reflect in part the nature of graduate education and in part the nature of graduate student demographics. Graduate students are older. They often have families and associated financial responsibilities that preclude continuous enrollment.

This pattern of lengthy stop-outs is probably more common in master's-level programs than it is in doctoral study, especially where there are no departmental or institutional time limits for completion of the master's degree. Doctoral candidates can "disappear" for a time, but the time not enrolled is usually limited by institutional policies specifying the amount of time that will be allowed between general examinations and completion of the degree. Extensions of time to complete the doctorate are usually possible, so that ultimately a successful degree candidate may actually not have enrolled for some number of years. In measuring retention, it may be necessary to make decisions about the handling of such cases. In general, it is necessary to set limits on nonenrollment to measure retention or attrition. These time limits may be dictated by university or program policy.

Retention. *Retention* generally refers to a student's continued enrollment. Retained students have not yet completed their studies, although students who received a degree can be counted as retained, as noted later. A complication arises with regard to graduate students.

The degree intent of graduate students is often difficult to determine from an institution's records. When a student enrolls in a master's program that does not lead to the doctorate, the intent can be reasonably assumed to be the master's degree, although the student may eventually pursue the doctorate in another program or at another institution. Completion of the master's degree can then be viewed as successful retention. When the student enrolls in a master's program leading to the doctoral degree, the intent is less obvious. Students applying to graduate programs have been sufficiently socialized to realize that they may decrease their chances of admission to doctoral programs by declaring the master's to be their final degree aspiration. Consequently, attrition from doctoral programs after attainment of the master's degree may not necessarily be attrition but rather fulfillment of the student's original degree plans. Decisions may be necessary about how to treat student intent in the computing of statistics on attrition and retention. However, if students indicate intent on an application form, they should be taken at their word, despite the inherent ambiguities.

Degree Completion. The ultimate formal educational goal of the graduate student is to complete a degree, whether it be the master's or the doctoral degree. Some graduate students may be involved in certificate programs or in nondegree or continuing education programs, and they probably should be treated separately or eliminated from discussions of retention. However, the problem in graduate education is the existence of multiple degrees. Again, assessment of master's and doctoral degree completion rates is complicated by student intent. From the perspective of measuring the productivity of a graduate program, degree completion would seem to be the bottom-line criterion. From a broader perspective, it would be of interest to know whether students who do not complete a degree at a given institution transfer to another and are successful there. However, such a follow-up study is beyond the scope of this discussion.

The Study of Retention

A number of variables are relevant to the study of graduate student retention. Some are simply demographic variables, such as gender, ethnicity, resident status (for example, in state, out of state, international), field of study, and age at entry. Others, such as undergraduate major or source of references, may be specific to program or institution. Still other variables—for example, undergraduate grade point average, Graduate Record Examination scores, type of undergraduate institution, previous degrees held—may be indexes of past performance.

The specific background variables selected will to some extent depend on the purposes of the retention study. If the principal purpose is to describe retention patterns at the institution, the background variables may differ from those of a study aimed at predicting future retention or evaluating graduate programs. In some cases, the background variables commonly collected in the usual admissions and registration process may suffice. In other cases—say, for a special study of retention—some of the data may come from specially designed survey instruments that may not be used on a regular basis (Girves and Wemmerus, 1988).

Measures of Retention

The criterion variables of interest will be those related to the completion of a degree or to continued enrollment. Several variables are worth consideration.

Completion Rates. The number of master's degrees, doctoral degrees, or both that graduate programs award comes close to what can be considered an appropriate criterion for measuring the instructional productivity of a graduate program. However, the number of graduates is confounded with the size of the program. Large programs tend to graduate large numbers of students. Thus, a completion ratio—the proportion of entering graduates (the entering cohort) who attain a particular degree (for example, the doctorate)—seems to be the most appropriate measure. Separate analyses can be conducted for other completion criteria. In doctoral programs, the proportion of the entering cohort passing general exams may be of interest as a criterion.

Bowen and Rudenstine (1992) discuss several measures of the completion rate. They define the minimum completion rate (MCR) as "the percentage of the entering cohort who have earned the doctorate by a specified year" (Bowen and Rudenstine, 1992, p. 106). For example, if the specified year is 1991, you will have an MCR for the cohort that entered in 1980, the cohort that entered in 1981, and so on, all relative to the year 1991. Obviously, the MCR tends to decline with each successive entering cohort, since students in the later cohorts have had less time to complete the degree. Bowen and Rudenstine discuss a second measure, the truncated completion rate (TCR), which they define as "the percentage of an entering cohort who earned the doctorate within a specified number of years from entry to graduate study" (Bowen and Rudenstine, 1992, p. 106). In this case, you select a critical number of years—say, six. Then you calculate the TCR for 1981 by computing the proportion of completions by 1987, the TCR for 1982 by computing the proportion of completions by 1988, and so on. The advantage of the TCR is that, when the most recent year is used as the specified year, it is not confounded by a decreasing number of elapsed years, as is the MCR. Obviously, you can compute MCRs and TCRs for master's programs as well.

A triangular representation can be used to present the results of an analysis that contains both the MCR and TCR measures. Such a representation is illustrated with hypothetical data in Table 2.1. The columns of the table show

Table 2.1. Triangular Representation

Entering Cohort Year	Graduation Cohort Year				
	1981	1982	1983	1984	1985
1980	.05	.10	.20	.45	.55
1981		.08	.11	.18	.40
1982			.10	.15	.41
1983				.11	.18
1984					.15

the MCR for a given year. For example, by 1985, 55 percent of the 1980 entering cohort had graduated, as had 40 percent of the 1981 entering cohort, 41 percent of the 1982 cohort, 18 percent of the 1983 entering cohort, and 15 percent of the 1984 entering cohort. As noted earlier, the MCR measure tends to decrease with each entering cohort, since fewer years have elapsed since time of entry. However, as the figures for the 1981 and 1982 entering cohorts show for the 1985 graduating cohort, the measure does not necessarily decrease, since different sets of students are involved.

The TCR measure can be read on the positive diagonal in Table 2.1. For example, if three years are chosen as the critical number of years, the TCR for 1980 is .20, .18 for 1981, and .41 for 1982. Although there is no obvious trend in the TCR for the three-year cutoff, there is a gradual upward trend in the one-year cutoff, as can be seen by following the positive diagonal of the table from upper left to lower right, that is, from .05 for the 1980 cohort to .15 for the 1984 cohort. Such a trend indicates that increasing numbers of students are completing their programs within the first year.

The triangular representation also shows the cumulative completion rate (CCR) for a given entering cohort for as many years as possible. The row for a given entering cohort shows the cumulative proportion of the entering cohort that completes the degree by the year represented by the column. For example, 5 percent of the 1980 entering cohort completed the degree by 1981, 20 percent completed the degree by 1983, and 55 percent completed the degree by 1985. Figure 2.1 plots CCRs for the data in Table 2.1. If data were available, the proportion of completions for a given entering cohort could be plotted against the number of years elapsed since entry. If you had sufficient years of data, the resulting plot would have an ogival form, gradually increasing for the first year or two, rapidly increasing for the next several years, and then gradually plateauing to the final completion rate for that year's cohort. As Bowen and Rudenstine (1992) point out, such plots can be useful in projecting time to degree, because the median time to degree corresponds to the number of years taken to attain half of the final completion rate. Such curves can be useful in comparing entering cohorts and fields of study.

Retention. Another measure of interest combines people in a given entering cohort who have attained the degree with those who are still enrolled at a given point in time. This index is perhaps the best measure of retention, because it excludes only those in an entering cohort who have neither enrolled in the program in the last year nor gotten the degree. The problem with the measure is that students who have not enrolled in a given year and who thus cannot be counted by this measure for the year may return in a subsequent year. Consequently, it is possible for this measure of retention to decline—as it should—and then to increase in a subsequent year because of returnees.

To return to the data in Table 2.1, cumulative completion rates for the 1980 entering cohort were .05, .10, .20, .45, and .55 for 1981, 1982, 1983, 1984, and 1985, respectively, as the first row shows. Suppose that 89 percent, 75 percent, 60 percent, 20 percent, and 5 percent had not attained a degree

Figure 2.1. Cumulative Completion Rates

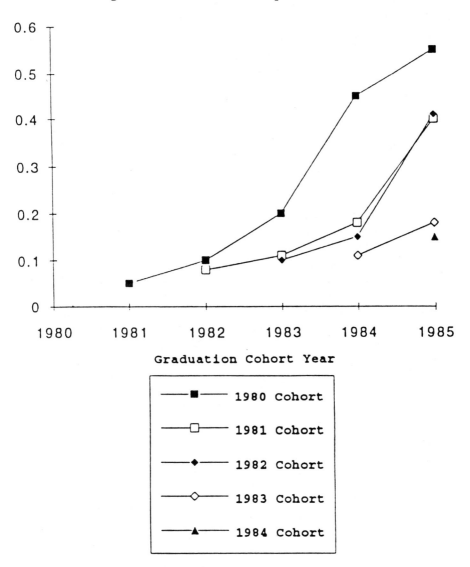

Graduation Cohort Year

and were still enrolled in the five years just named. The proportion retained (PR) measure is the sum of the CCR and the proportion still enrolled for the year: .94, .85, .80, .65, and .60 for the five years under study. These figures give the proportion of students who are still enrolled or who have already completed the degree in question. A triangular representation for this measure can be constructed as well. An alternative retention measure would count only students still enrolled. However, the alternative measure does not give credit for successful completions.

Studying Retention Among Master's and Doctoral Students

The preceding discussion indicates how various measures of completion and retention can be computed for a given entering cohort. However, the issue of degree completed has only been discussed generically. That is, you can compute the MCR or the TCR for either the master's degree or the doctorate. Thus, for a given entering cohort, you can annually compute MCRs for the doctorate and the master's. Or, if you define success simply as the attainment of some degree, you can compute an MCR for either degree. However, including master's and doctoral degree students in the same analysis can be misleading if doctoral completion and retention are at issue. Note that you can compute these statistics to obtain universitywide figures or separate figures for each graduate program.

Program-Level Analysis. At the level of an individual graduate program, the distinction between master's and doctoral retention is easy to resolve. For example, students can be admitted into a terminal master's program or into a doctoral program. In each case, entering cohorts are students seeking the master's or students seeking the doctoral degree, and separate analyses can be conducted for the two groups. Degree intent, if the data are available, may also be relevant in determining the cohort. If the master's degree is a way station to the doctorate, completion of the doctorate is the final criterion for success. However, it may be of interest to compute the proportion of the entering cohort who attain the master's, or the master's and general exam, or the master's and doctorate; or the general exam in master's/doctorate programs; or the general exam and doctorate in doctorate-only programs. The proportion retained (PR) measure—earned degree or still enrolled—could also be computed. The measure or measures that are appropriate should be determined at the program level. Several measures, when combined with time-to-degree analyses, may be instructive.

Institutional-Level Analyses. Institutional-level analyses are complicated by the fact that any institution has a variety of master's and doctoral programs. If all programs are doctoral or if all programs are master's, the analyses are straightforward. A mixture of programs requires several approaches. Master's-only programs can be combined and analyzed separately from master's/doctorate programs. The master's/doctorate and doctorate-only programs can be combined, and the doctoral degree can be taken as the criterion for computation of MCR and TCR. In the master's/doctorate programs, degree intent data can be used to identify entering cohorts, that is, master's-degree-only or eventual doctorate. In doctoral or master's/doctorate programs, passing the general exam may also serve as a criterion of success and be analyzed separately.

Clearly, a number of analyses are possible. The analysis chosen will depend on the needs of the program or institution. All require definition of an entering cohort (for example, students pursuing the master's, students pursuing the doctorate) and a retention criterion measure (for example, attainment of the master's degree, attainment of the doctoral degree, passing general exams, or still being enrolled). Then an MCR, a TCR, both an MCR and a TCR, or a PR success measure can be computed for each entering cohort for each criterion to determine the proportion of students in a given cohort who satisfy the criterion by a given year.

Who Are the Players?

A retention study may be easier to describe in the abstract than to implement in a specific program or institution. The goal is to get the relevant data recorded in a common file that can then be analyzed. The organization of a specific institution and its data management practices determine who must be involved in creating a data base that can be used to study retention. The discussion that follows suggests the kinds of problems that can arise because different offices have differing responsibilities.

Admissions. Admissions staff is usually the first point of official contact between the student and the institution. Individual institutions give the admissions function differing roles and organize it in different ways. However, the admissions staff is usually the first to enter information about prospective students in university records. At some institutions, information entered into computer files by admissions staff is subsequently transferred to files on enrolled students, with or without editing. If there are errors during initial data entry, they may be perpetuated in permanent student records. In addition, the admissions staff is sometimes placed in the position of determining the information that will be collected on application forms. Consultation with the graduate office and others interested in retention should help to ensure that the necessary information is obtained and that there is agreement about where and by whom the data should be stored and entered.

Registrar. The registrar's office keeps a variety of information on enrolled students. Information collected by admissions staff may in large part be transferred to the registrar after the student enrolls. However, some of the information may be subject to change after the student has been enrolled for a time. For example, the admissions data may contain information on the degree intended at the time of admission. However, once the student passes the master's hurdle, the registrar may change that indication in the student's record unless the registrar has specifically been instructed not to change the record from master's degree intended to doctoral. Name changes can also create problems. Coordination among the various offices will be necessary, and the institutional research staff may be the natural coordinators if they know which information is needed and who controls the records that contain it.

Graduate School. In some cases, the graduate school is the best repository of the necessary information on graduate students. Further, the graduate school may be the only office on campus with certain kinds of information, for example, on the time and outcome of doctoral general (or qualifying) exams.

Obviously, the resources of the graduate school will limit its capability to store and analyze relevant data, and institutional research staff may be expected to conduct the analyses. When a graduate school has its own computer capability, the preparation of data needed for the analysis of retention may involve relatively little, since the data stored for regular graduate student monitoring and record keeping contain much of what one needs. Some of these data may duplicate information retained by the registrar. However, downloading from one system to another may be possible, and the savings in speed of access to the graduate student records may well be worth the duplication. Moreover, the graduate schools are often called on for information about graduate students, and they should be in the best position to identify variables that are relevant to institutional research on graduate students.

Graduate Program or Department. Individual programs or departments may well be in the best position to provide accurate, relevant data on individual graduate students. However, departments also vary widely in their capability and interest in keeping accurate, up-to-date records on a data base that can be used for analysis. Moreover, departments are likely to differ in the information that they think is important to store and in the ways in which they define variables and counting rules. So, while departments may be the only source for certain kinds of information, the data required for maintenance of retention records are usually available elsewhere.

Institutional Research Office. The institutional research office may be linked to central university data bases and have adequate programming and analysis support to conduct basic retention analyses. The problems most likely to result from relying on an institution-level office is that staff does not necessarily know the details of graduate student variables relevant to retention issues. For example, the institutional research office may be able to provide data tracking students who first enrolled in a given year. However, institutional research staff may not be aware that not all students are degree-seeking students. For example, graduate nondegree students take courses for personal satisfaction or reasons of professional advancement. The institution may or may not have an official category for these students. Retention data that include these students will underestimate the completion rate for degree-seeking students. Thus, it is essential to include persons familiar with the issues unique to graduate education in the planning of any retention studies conducted by an institutional research office and to update institutional research staff on changes in policies that can affect their analyses.

Personnel Office. Some data relevant to the study of retention may be held in the university's personnel office. For example, information about the financial support history of students, including information about their service as teaching or research assistants, may be relevant to a study of factors contributing to retention of graduate students. If the personnel office maintains its own data base, collaboration with this office will be necessary to gain access to the data.

What Do You Need to Know About Students?

In order to study completion and retention rates, some information, such as entry and completion dates, is essential. Further, it may be important to examine rates for different subgroups. However, if the intent is to examine factors contributing to retention and degree completion, data on other variables should also be collected. These variables can then be used in equations, such as multiple regression analyses, to predict completion within some criterion number of years. Table 2.2 relates variables that will be helpful in the study of retention to the offices that may have that information. Variables that are essential for the study of retention have been asterisked.

Table 2.2.   Variables for a Retention Study

Variable	A	D	FA	GS	Pr	R	Rs
			Potential Source of Information				
Name of program*	X	X		X		X	
Entry date to degree program*	X	X		X		X	
Degree sought*	X	X		X		X	
Previous degrees*	X	X		X		X	
Enrollment status by quarter or semester*		X		X		X	
Full-time, part-time status						X	
Active in program but not enrolled*		X					
Degree date for master's*				X		X	
Degree date for doctorate*				X		X	
Date general exam taken and passed				X			
Field of study*	X			X		X	
Gender*	X			X		X	
Ethnicity*	X			X		X	
Residence Status*	X			X		X	
Credit hours accumulated at each quarter or semester of enrollment						X	
Undergraduate grade point average	X						
Cumulative grade point average						X	
Graduate Record Examination scores	X					X	
Number of quarters (semesters) on fellowship		X	X	X			
Number of quarters (semesters) on graduate assistantship (TA and RA as separate variables)		X		X	X		X
Other variables deemed appropriate for the individual setting							

Note: A = admissions; D = department; FA = financial aid; GS = graduate school; Pr = personnel office; R = registrar; Rs = office of research. Essential variables are asterisked (*).

Some of the variables listed in Table 2.2 require coding options. For example, degree sought may have several options, dictated by the practice of the institution, for example, master's, tagged master's, doctorate, tagged doctorate, or no degree. For some analyses, the no degree student may be excluded.

The more serious problem is that, when several offices have information on a given variable, their records may not be in agreement. The registrar's office is generally the official source for the information that it retains, even if other offices have information of their own. In addition, some information will change over time, and the responsibility for updating the information must be settled. Coordination and agreement will be needed among offices on these issues. The institutional research office should play an important role in identifying issues and helping to resolve them. However, no single office, especially in large institutions, is likely to have all the information needed to proceed without consultation. The relevant graduate school should have the final say on how official data on graduate students should be coded, although in most cases the options will be fairly clear. If the parties cannot agree, the office of academic affairs may have to intervene.

Construction of a Retention Data Base

Eventually, a data base must be constructed that can be used for the study of retention. The institutional research staff should design and construct the data base in consultation with other offices. Responsibilities for entering the data can be shared, but some fairly obvious demarcations can be identified: Any data collected prior to enrollment should be entered by the admissions staff, whether departmental or in a central office. The central office staff may maintain its own data base, from which institutional research staff can download relevant data to the retention data base. If departmental staff enter data directly into a central data base, care must be taken to ensure that everyone agrees on definitions and options.

As noted earlier, standard information on enrolled students is usually the responsibility of the registrar. The graduate school will have information on graduate exams. The graduate school or central personnel office should have information on fellowship or graduate assistant positions, although in some cases a department or the graduate school may have information not available to the central office. The department may also be able to help if a distinction is made between students who are actually enrolled and those who, while not enrolled, are still viewed as active in the program. It may be desirable to have a uniform definition of *active,* but fields vary, and forcing uniformity may be inappropriate or unrealistic.

The institutional research (IR) office may have to coordinate the activities of different offices to ensure that data are in fact being entered. (Missing data problems can be vexing.) If a single IR office handles all data integrity problems, consistency is more easily managed. Further, the IR office should make sure that it is communicating with the graduate school concerning changes in graduate school policies (for example, how does the graduate school define *full-time student*, and does the definition vary for graduate assistants and fellows?) and the unique characteristics of graduate students (for example, how do graduate nondegree students differ from conditional admissions?). The IR office needs to be aware of graduate school practices in response to external reporting requirements that lead to variances from university definitions as well. Similarly, the graduate school may wish to be involved in determining how to handle intra- and extrauniversity transfers. When a student changes programs within the university—for example, from psychology to anthropology—should psychology count the student as an attrition and anthropology as a new admission, and should starting dates be reset? The answers depend on the goal of the analysis, but all records should be kept, including records of the change of programs. How should previous graduate degrees from other institutions be counted? (They should probably be counted only by noting what the previous degree was in.)

The graduate school also may be the only office that has information on the date of the general exam and its outcome. For doctoral students, the general exam is clearly a critical point, and any study of retention should include information on the general exam. Attrition between the master's degree and the general exam or between the general exam and completion of the doctorate cannot be studied if information about the general exam is not available.

Conclusion

Although relatively little attention has been paid to the measurement of retention, it is increasingly important to gauge the success rates of graduate programs. Time to degree is an important variable, and it has received a good bit of attention. The investment of time and resources in students who do not complete degree programs is another serious matter. Degree completion rates can help to identify problem areas in graduate programs requiring further examination and improvement.

References

Bowen, W. G., and Rudenstine, N. L. *In Pursuit of the Ph.D.* Princeton, N.J.: Princeton University Press, 1992.

Council of Graduate Schools Task Force. *The Doctor of Philosophy Degree.* Washington, D.C.: Council of Graduate Schools, 1990.

Girves, J. E., and Wemmerus, V. "Developing Models of Graduate Student Degree Progress." *Journal of Higher Education,* 1988, 59 (2), 163–189.

Middleton, E. J., and Mason, E. J. (eds.). *Recruitment and Retention of Minority Students in Teacher Education: Proceedings of the National Invitational Conference.* Lexington: University of Kentucky, 1987.

PAUL D. ISAAC is associate dean of the Graduate School at The Ohio State University, Columbus.

How the University of California at Berkeley's graduate division has used quantitative analysis and qualitative methods to address the issues of time to doctoral degree and student retention is described. The graduate division used this research to develop recommendations and design programmatic outreach activities to improve graduate education.

From Facts to Action: Expanding the Graduate Division's Educational Role

Maresi Nerad, Joseph Cerny

Mounting concern over the anticipated shortage of college teachers, scientists, and engineers and society's need to diversify faculty has made time to doctoral degree and doctoral completion major issues for graduate deans, funding agencies, and government officials. As a result, for the last several years the graduate division at the University of California at Berkeley has studied doctoral completion times and rates. Breaking out of its traditional administrative role, the graduate division undertook research and used its findings to design and implement programs that encourage students to complete their degrees and to do so in a reasonable amount of time. This chapter describes how the University of California at Berkeley's graduate division used quantitative analysis and qualitative methods to address the issues of time to doctoral degree and student retention. It shows how graduate schools and other administrative units can conduct similar research and use its results to develop recommendations and design programmatic outreach activities to improve graduate education.

Our Berkeley study proceeded in five steps: First, we developed a number of statistical analyses based on demographic data on our graduate students to determine the average time to degree in each Ph.D. program, the completion rates, and the points in these programs at which students tended to leave without completing their doctoral degrees. Second, we compared the Berkeley data with national trends and with the results of similar analyses at

The data used in this study were produced by the staff of the Information and Technology unit of the Berkeley Graduate Division—Betty Liu, Bob Tidd, and Dennis Anderson—under the direction of Judi Sui. Jim Litrownik and Joyce Travlos produced the data from the National Research Council tapes of doctorates earned on the nine University of California campuses.

comparable institutions. Third, we interviewed and surveyed students in an attempt to find the reasons for long time to degree and low completion rates in certain disciplines. Fourth, by combining the knowledge accumulated from quantitative and qualitative findings, we developed a conceptual model to determine the conditions under which students completed their degrees in good time and with a low rate of attrition. Fifth, we used this model as the basis for developing policies and making recommendations to the graduate council of the Berkeley academic senate, faculty, graduate students, and graduate assistants and secretaries on ways of shortening time to degree and increasing completion rates.

Time to Doctoral Degree

The average time to degree from entrance to Berkeley for all our doctoral recipients receiving degrees between July 1980 and June 1987 ($N = 4,949$) was 6.9 years. This figure includes the time students spent earning a master's degree if it was required for the Ph.D. It also includes the time during which students were not registered and were perhaps away from the campus.

As expected, we found that time to degree varied widely by field of study. Berkeley groups the various Ph.D. programs into eight major fields of study: arts, biological sciences, engineering, languages and literature, natural resources, physical sciences, professional schools, and social sciences. No law (J.D.) data were included. The most substantial differences in mean time to doctorate occurred between students in engineering (5.5 years) and the natural sciences (6.0 to 6.2 years) on the one hand and students in the social sciences (8.4 years), arts (8.6 years), and languages and literature (8.9 years) on the other. We did not see substantial differences between minority and non-minority students or between men and women. Foreign students across disciplines completed their degrees more quickly than domestic students.

Completion Rates

Our most recent analysis of completion rates utilizes additional data from the cohorts entering in 1978 and 1979 as measured in November 1989. Only students who identified themselves as working toward the doctoral degree at entrance were included. Fifty-eight percent of the students in the 1978 and 1979 cohorts completed doctoral degrees. Another 20 percent changed their plans, earned master's degrees, and left graduate school. Thus, a total of 78 percent completed a graduate degree of some kind. Doctoral completion rates varied markedly by major field of study. The biological sciences (72 percent) and physical sciences (69 percent) had the highest completion rates. The arts (39 percent) and languages and literature (37 percent) had the lowest. Percentages in the other four fields were 48 percent for the professional schools, 49 percent for social sciences, and 65 percent for both engineering and natural resources.

When analyzing data by sex, race, and ethnicity, one has to be aware that women and non-Asian minority students are more heavily represented in fields where long time to degree and low completion rates are the norm—the professional schools, social sciences, and humanities. Unfortunately, statistically meaningful data on minorities for this data set are not available at this point. However, when women as a group are compared with men as a group, the completion rates within major fields differ significantly. Women overall had a completion rate of 47 percent, while men had a completion rate of 63 percent.

Contrary to popular belief, the majority of the graduate students who failed to earn the doctorate left the program before advancement to candidacy for the Ph.D., not after. Although 24 percent of the students in the 1978 and 1979 cohorts left during their first three years of graduate study, most of these students (83 percent) earned the master's degree. An additional 10 percent left after advancement to candidacy, and another 8 percent were pending at the time when we analyzed the data.

Comparison with Other Universities

Is the situation just outlined unique to Berkeley? In the second step of our study, we compared our current sample with other universities. National Research Council data show that, during the last twenty years, time to degree, both at Berkeley and nationally, appears to be increasing. We asked the University of Michigan at Ann Arbor to work with us on a comparison of our doctoral time to degree and completion rates. For the 1975–1976 and 1977–79 cohorts, both Berkeley and Michigan found that slightly more than half of all their doctoral students had completed their degrees in a period of seven years. Ellen Benkin's (1984) study at the University of California at Los Angeles (UCLA) showed that about 30 percent of UCLA students leave during the early period of the doctoral studies. These comparisons showed that Berkeley was not atypical, at least among public universities.

Reasons for Lengthy Time to Degree

Third, we asked, Why do some students leave a doctoral program? Why do some take longer than seems appropriate? To answer these questions, we began qualitative research, mainly in-depth interviews.

Initially, we interviewed forty University of California at Berkeley students from history, English, French, and sociology in ninety-minute individual interviews. We chose these departments because our analysis showed that students historically took a long time and had low completion rates in these departments. For comparison, we interviewed students from psychology and biochemistry. All these students had nearly completed their dissertation or had just filed their theses. About half of the students took at least one year longer than the average departmental time to degree; the other half completed in average time.

The interviews walked the students through the five major stages of the doctoral program: course work; preparation for the oral qualifying exam; finding a dissertation topic, selecting a dissertation adviser, and writing a prospectus; researching and writing the dissertation; and applying for professional employment. Students were asked how they had moved from one stage to the next, what financial and moral support they had had, what would have helped them at each stage, and what the university could do to help students finish more quickly.

Results

We found six major patterns for students in the humanities and social sciences who had long time to degree.

First, students in departments that required an M.A. thesis spent an excessive amount of time polishing the master's thesis. They seemed to receive mixed messages from the faculty. They were told to do a simple thesis, and simultaneously they were told to choose a topic with potential so they could get their feet wet in "real research." In addition to the pressure to produce, they hoped to increase their chances for receiving a fellowship by writing an impressive master's thesis.

Second, students in the humanities and social sciences overprepared for their orals. They spent, on the average, from six months to one year studying, usually in isolation and withdrawn from the department. Their ideas about the structure, scope, and standards of the exam were vague. The mystery that surrounded the exam seemed to lead to a self-imposed perfectionism. After taking the exam, they were disappointed to discover that they had been given an opportunity to demonstrate only a small part of their knowledge.

Third, after passing the qualifying exam, these students spent between one and two years searching for a dissertation topic and writing a dissertation prospectus. They did not have information about the prospectus format; they knew only how long it should be. They had difficulty deciding which topics were feasible and which goals were achievable within a certain period of time.

Fourth, students in the humanities and social sciences wrote their dissertations in total isolation. They felt lost in the transition between what they called a *class-taking person* and a *book-writing person*. During this period, they completely withdrew from departmental activities. Most said, "No one on the faculty knows about my topic, so why should I meet with them?" During the actual writing period, they found it very difficult to work as a teaching assistant or at an unrelated on- or off-campus job.

Fifth, students who took longer than expected to obtain their degrees perceived the course work, orals, and prospectus-writing stages of their doctoral studies as hurdles that needed to be jumped, not as steps leading to completion of their dissertations. The curriculum structure was not seen as an opportunity to develop an overview of their field and to decide on a research project. As a result, the students focused too narrowly on getting the course requirements out of the way or on taking the orals for the orals' sake. After passing their orals, they had trouble mustering the energy needed to write a dissertation proposal. In fact, they felt that they were starting from scratch as they approached the proposal writing. When their proposal had been approved, they often realized that they needed to take more courses in the area of their dissertation topic.

Sixth, many humanities and social science students complained that the department and faculty failed to help them prepare for orals, develop a dissertation prospectus, apply for grants, or write their dissertations. Further, students found that it was very difficult to find work after advancement to candidacy and that, if they were employed as a teaching or research assistant, it was distracting to be doing work unrelated to their theses.

A study conducted by Nerad (1991) for the nine UC campuses revealed similar patterns for students in the humanities and social sciences who took a long time to complete their degree programs.

Working Model of Factors Determining Time to Degree and Attrition

After gaining insight into some reasons why students in the humanities and social sciences took a long time to complete the doctorate, we asked students why they left the doctoral program before completing the degree. As expected, substantial numbers of students left for both personal and institutional reasons.

Personal Reasons. Students who left graduate school after one or two years often reported that their expectations about the general field of study, graduate student life, or the focus of the program had not been met. Students, particularly in the professional schools and engineering who already had a master's degree, rethought their career goals and chose to leave, often after the first year. These students could return to well-paying jobs as an alternative to jumping the many hurdles in graduate school.

Institutional Reasons. By pulling together what we had learned from our qualitative data on departments at the extreme ends of our variables of interest, we developed the model shown in Table 3.1 to interpret institutional conditions that affect time to degree and attrition rates. The model was organized around nine points: research mode, program structure, definition of the dissertation, departmental advising, departmental environment, availability of research money, financial support, campus facilities, and the job market. With the help of this model, the graduate division could begin to determine where we might recommend or implement programs to assist doctoral students.

Research Mode. Research mode is a field-specific factor. There are pronounced differences between the sciences and humanities in the way in which research is conducted. Graduate students in the sciences and engineering acquire research skills through an apprenticeship mode of research instruction and teamwork in a laboratory setting where they benefit from frequent social

Table 3.1. Institutional and Field-Specific Factors Determining Time to Degree

	Short Time/Low Attrition	*Long Time/High Attrition*
Research Mode	Apprenticeship Teamwork Laboratory	Individualistic learning Solitariness Library
Program Structure	No M.A./M.S. required Qualifying exam includes dissertation prospectus Annual evaluation	M.A./M.S. required Qualifying exam does not include dissertation prospectus Sporadic Evaluations
Definition of the Dissertation	Test of future ability to do research	Contribution to existing knowledge
Departmental Advising	Faculty mentoring Departmental advising	Absence of faculty mentoring and department advising
Departmental Environment	Sense of community Students treated as junior colleagues Student participation in department administration	Factions among faculty Students treated as adolescents No student participation in department administration
Research Money	Many sources	Few sources
Type of Financial Support	Research assistantships Fellowships	Teaching assistantships Loans
Campus Facilities Housing Child care Space Transportation Library	 Affordable Available Available (office, meeting) Efficient, affordable Long hours, year round	 Expensive Overcrowded Overcrowded Slow, expensive Short summer hours
Job Market Postdoctoral Academic Industry	Many openings Good salaries	Few openings Low salaries

interactions. The laboratory research and the dissertation work often coincide, and they are often supported by a research assistantship under the direction of a faculty investigator. In contrast, the arts, humanities, social sciences, and professional schools do not have the same structure for involving students as active participants in the research process. In addition, these fields have few resources to pay for research assistants. Although the research mode plays an important role in retaining students in a doctoral program and helping them to complete the program in a timely manner, this factor is not one that can be altered by administrative intervention from the graduate division.

Program Structure. Program structure emerged as a strong determinant in interviews with students. Requiring a master's degree of the student who seeks a doctorate affects time to degree. To investigate this point further, we used data for all nine University of California (UC) campuses that the National Research Council (NRC) had gathered in its annual survey of earned doctorates. We rearranged these data into three groups: students who did not receive a master's, students who received the master's and the doctorate at the same institution, and students who received the master's degree at an institution other than the doctoral-granting institution. The findings are not surprising. Students with no master's degree take the shortest time (6.0 years), while students with the master's from another institution take the longest time (9.8 years), since the doctoral-granting institution rarely accepts a substantial portion of the prior course work. Students who enter a doctoral program with a master's degree from another institution often take more courses voluntarily in order to become familiar with the faculty. Students with a master's degree from the same institution complete the program in less time than those who come with master's degrees from another institution, but they take longer than those with no master's degree (7.4 years). Seventy percent of all UC students acquired a master's degree before the doctorate, half (35 percent) at the campus from which they received the doctorate, half (35 percent) from a different institution.

A survey at Berkeley found that programs requiring a dissertation prospectus as part of the qualifying examination tended to have shorter time to degree. (Some life science programs even had students write this prospectus as a grant proposal.) Programs with a structure that called for an early start to dissertation research tended to have shorter times to degree. Programs that evaluated students' progress annually and suggested improvements seemed to give students confidence about completing the degree. Students especially appreciated the regular progress meetings with dissertation committees after advancement to candidacy; these students appeared to drift less.

Definition of the Dissertation. Another factor affecting time to degree is whether the dissertation is perceived primarily as a test of future ability to do research or as a book. Science and engineering programs generally seem to perceive the dissertation as a test of future ability to do research. Humanities and social sciences programs often expect the dissertation to be a major contribution to the field.

Departmental Advising. Because the concept of advising is broad, we broke it into two components: advising and mentoring by the individual dissertation director and advising and guidance by the department as a whole. Where departmental advising activities exist, there is some guarantee that things just do not happen accidentally or never at all, and students tend to receive more direction and drift less.

To obtain further insight into students' satisfaction with advising, we examined the graduate division's exit questionnaire, which is required at the time when the dissertation is filed. (The return rate is 95 percent.) One question is, How satisfied have you been with departmental advising? Responses from 1,200 students who completed their dissertation between fall 1987 and fall 1988 show that about half were satisfied, one-quarter were very satisfied, and one-quarter were dissatisfied. The level of satisfaction varied significantly by major fields. Social science and humanities students were the least satisfied. Physical science, engineering, and natural resources students were the most satisfied. Proportionally more women than men were dissatisfied, although the difference was not statistically significant.

Another relevant question asked was, How satisfied have you been with the professional relationship with your dissertation adviser? Here, the overall satisfaction level was considerably higher, since more than 92 percent reported that they were satisfied with their adviser. Interestingly, students in the social sciences were more satisfied with their individual advisers than students in the biological sciences, and humanities students were the most satisfied. Again, women were more dissatisfied than men. From the interviews, we found that students had good personal relationships with their advisers, but many did not receive enough professional support. Students expected an adviser to be a mentor who would set standards, develop their skills, advise them on appropriate and feasible dissertation topics, and treat them as junior colleagues.

Departmental Environment. What impact does the environment in the department have on time to degree and attrition rates? Some departments were identified as having an impersonal environment that provided no professional student support activities or social events or that recognized only star students, leaving others with the sense that they were failures. In these departments, students were likely to take a longer time to degree or to leave before completing the doctoral degree. The climate within a department is often linked with the kind of advising available. Departments that support their students with programs designed to assist them at each stage of the doctoral program and with social gatherings may have a lower attrition rate. This is an area in which more research is necessary.

Availability of Research Money. According to students, faculty, and many graduate deans, one key factor influencing time to degree is financial support for doctoral students. Many students in the arts, humanities, and social sciences are affected adversely because the few faculty research grants that might also support students are small. However, most students in engineering, physical sciences, and biological sciences can count on employment as research assistants, employment that is supported by their faculty member's research grants. In many cases, that work constitutes their dissertation research as well.

Type of Financial Support. We did a one-time study of the relationship between time to degree and financial support per individual student. For this study, the unit of analysis was the actual expenses and financial support of each student who completed a degree between May 1986 and May 1989 in three social sciences and two humanities fields. We assume that these five departments had an equal proportion of outstanding students—all five departments rank among the top seven programs in the nation in their respective disciplines. First, the financial support was calculated during each student's first five years by amount and length of time of each type of support. These figures were then compared with the time that students took to complete their degrees. Students who received between four and five years of support took the shortest time to degree—an average of 7.9 years—while those who received no support took twice as long—16.6 years. As expected, time to degree decreased with an increase in support.

Second, the annual (twelve-month) financial support was divided by the annual (twelve-month) expenses. (The annual student expenses were taken from the student financial aid budgets of the appropriate year; these budgets were extrapolated to twelve months.) The results of these calculations showed that, on the average, support money could cover between 30 percent and 90 percent of a student's expenses during his or her first five years in the program. Departments varied in the type of support that they gave to students and in the length of time for which the support was provided. Not surprisingly, the department offering the most financial support had the shortest time to degree. The department that offered the most financial support in the form of teaching assistantships had an intermediate time to degree. Significantly, the department with shortest time to degree not only provided the most financial support but distributed the support most equally among research assistantships, teaching assistantships, and fellowships. From these results, we can reconfirm that time to degree is related to the amount and type of support that students receive, but we must also emphasize that, in the humanities and social sciences, factors other than financial support, particularly the structure of the Ph.D. program, also significantly influence time to degree.

We also examined the relationship between time to degree and the number of years for which students were supported by teaching assistantships in these five departments. The study showed that students who taught three or more years took one year longer (9.9) to complete the degree than students who taught less than three years (8.8). Given these findings, the graduate division would recommend that, if at all possible, humanities and social science departments implement a support package that gave students an efficient mix of support for each stage of the doctoral program—fellowships for the first year, teaching assistantships for years two and three, fellowships at the conceptualizing stage of the dissertation, and, if available, research assistantships and a dissertation-writing fellowship for the final two years.

Campus Facilities. The quality and effectiveness of the library, the availability of office and meeting space, and issues of transportation, housing, and child care certainly can influence time to degree. Of particular concern are housing and child care costs and availability for students with dependents. In order to shed some light on time to degree issues for students with dependents,

Table 3.2.   Effect of Dependents on Mean Time (Years) to Degree

Student Group	One or More Dependents	No Dependents	Difference	Difference Women/Men
Men (all)	9.1 yrs.	7.6	1.5	
With dependents	47%			
				0.7
Women (all)	11.3	9.1	· 2.2	
With dependents	29%			
White	9.8	8.3	1.5	
With dependents	37%			
Asian	9.2	7.5	1.7	
With dependents	45%			
African American	12.5	11.4	1.1	
With dependents	48%			
Chicano/Latino	9.7	8.6	1.1	
With dependents	55%			
Total	9.5	8.2	1.3	
With dependents	42%			

we used the NRC data on earned doctorates, disaggregating doctoral recipients with dependents from doctoral recipients without dependents. We then correlated time to degree with dependent status. As Table 3.2 shows, of the 1980–88 doctoral recipients on the nine UC campuses, 42 percent had one or more dependents. Men and women with dependents took 1.5 and 2.2 years longer, respectively, than recipients with no dependents. In addition, minority graduate students at UC have a higher percentage of dependents than white students, so the availability and affordability of housing and child care may be particularly important for retention of these students. The fact that child-care facilities are inadequate on most campuses poses a real problem if we want to attract more women and minority students to our doctoral programs.

Job Market. Faculty most often cite the lack of academic jobs as a major reason for high attrition and the lengthening time to degree in some disciplines. This factor is beyond the control of the university. However, departments, faculty, and administrative units, such as career planning and placement centers, can actively support students in their job search. Departments can offer seminars that address the various aspects of becoming a professional in one's field and prepare students for national conferences at which job interviews are held. Departments can also appoint faculty placement officers.

Developing Recommendations

As our last step, we developed recommendations and the graduate division designed and implemented activities aimed at decreasing time to degree and lowering attrition. In this process, we worked with faculty, graduate students, and graduate assistants and secretaries. Finally, many of these recommendations were developed in conjunction with the graduate council of Berkeley's academic senate.

Faculty. We initiated a monthly invitational seminar on graduate education at Berkeley. Membership in the group of thirty-five included faculty and department chairs, senior administrators from the Berkeley campus and the UC systemwide office, members from the graduate council (the legislative arm of graduate education at Berkeley), graduate students, senior graduate assistants, and the several deans of the graduate division. The seminar had multiple goals: to inform and sensitize a part of the campus community, particularly the faculty, to these issues of graduate education; to generate ideas on changes that should be made; and to gather feedback on recommendations that we had developed.

Administrators in the graduate division also met monthly with faculty and students who served on an ad hoc subcommittee of the graduate council to develop appropriate recommendations. Last year, one focus of these meetings was to formulate a new policy requiring students to meet annually with at least two members of their dissertation committee to review their progress on their dissertation and map out a plan for the following year. This annual review is designed to improve communication between students and their committees and to provide students with feedback on their work.

In addition, the dean of the graduate division sent a data packet to each department. The data packet included information on time to degree and completion for each department at Berkeley, the frequency distribution of departmental time to degree, a list of department faculty with the average time to Ph.D. of their advisees during the last ten years, and some key results from the doctoral student exit questionnaire. The dean asked each department's senior graduate advisers to identify steps that the department had been taking or could take, if appropriate, to improve the situation for its graduate students.

Graduate Students. We initiated meetings with interdepartmental student focus groups. The best ideas emerged from these focus groups. During each semester, we met once a month with a group of twelve to fifteen doctoral candidates from various departments within one major field of study. These meetings served several purposes. First, they functioned as a support group for the students, giving them a chance to recognize that others shared the same difficulties and worries and making them aware of what other departments were doing for their students. Second, these sessions told students that their problems were being taken seriously, helped to develop possible solutions with them, and encouraged them to initiate departmental support activities. Third, the graduate division improved its understanding of the specific needs of students and received ideas about educational activities that we could offer or that we could encourage the department or other campus units to provide.

From the student focus group emerged the idea of a workshop sponsored by the graduate division on practical tips for dissertation writing. The information packet that we are now distributing to all doctoral students when they advance to candidacy originated in the focus group meetings. This packet is intended to help students make the transition more easily from taking classes to doing research and writing. The packet contains a question-and-answer sheet relating to major problems that may arise for a doctoral candidate; reprints from our graduate student newsletter on choosing a dissertation topic, writing a successful grant proposal, and writing the thesis; and a list of services for Ph.D. students seeking academic employment.

The graduate division also sponsored an annual faculty forum entitled "The View from the Other Side of the Desk." At this forum, faculty discuss how they see their role as dissertation advisers and their opinions regarding the purpose of the dissertation.

Graduate Assistants. We formed an advisory group of graduate assistants whose function is similar to that of the student focus groups: They exchange information about shared problems, develop ideas and recommendations, and reflect on implementation of these recommendations. Close collegial contact with the graduate assistants is essential since they are important to the actual implementation of our policies. In addition, the graduate division (Graduate Division, 1992) produced a resource guide for departments based on successful departmental activities currently offered to graduate students. This guide provides departments with ideas for student support activities.

The activities that we have described were possible for three reasons: A professional position was created in the graduate division, the publication unit was expanded to include a full range of outreach activities in addition to publications aimed at helping students succeed in graduate school, and our information and technology unit was able to develop ways of using our historical data base to address pressing issues in doctoral education.

Conclusion

To summarize, this chapter describes how the graduate division on the Berkeley campus of the University of California has used various research activities to address the issues of time to doctoral degree and doctoral student retention with a focus on their improvement. We have supplemented quantitative analyses with qualitative methods to develop a basis for designing recommendations and programmatic outreach activities. This approach—working with the academic senate, faculty, graduate students, and graduate assistants—has increased awareness of the issues to be resolved and dedication to their resolution. It has also demonstrated that a graduate division—part of the administration—can also function as an educational agency, not exclusively as a bureaucratic unit.

References

Benkin, E. "Where Have All the Doctoral Students Gone: A Study of Doctoral Attrition at U.C.L.A." Unpublished doctoral dissertation, University of California, Los Angeles, 1984.

Graduate Division. *Easing the Way for Graduate Students.* Berkeley: Graduate Division, University of California, 1992.

Nerad, M. *Graduate Education at the University of California and Factors Affecting Time-to-Degree.* Berkeley: Graduate Division, University of California, 1991.

MARESI NERAD, who has a Ph.D. in higher education, is responsible for research in the Graduate Division at the University of California, Berkeley.

JOSEPH CERNY is professor of chemistry, provost for research, and dean of the Graduate Division at the University of California, Berkeley.

The use of structural modeling to study graduate education and address policy questions is discussed. The method is illustrated in a step-by-step example.

Examining Graduate Education Through Structural Modeling

Amaury Nora, Alberto F. Cabrera

This chapter provides a basic introduction to the use of structural modeling in the study of graduate education–related processes. The intended audience consists of institutional researchers and policy makers seeking basic information about how structural modeling can be used to address policy questions involving processes, to study the role of specific components in causal models of graduate education, and to develop new ways of measuring constructs in graduate education—that is, of validating scales used to measure different outcomes.

The chapter does not focus on the mathematical foundations underlying structural modeling. These foundations have been discussed in detail by Pedhazur (1982), Joreskog and Sorbom (1989a, 1989b), Bentler (1989), and Muthen (1988), among others. Rather, it emphasizes how to interpret the results of statistical software aimed at testing structures. Accordingly, the chapter is organized into six sections. The first two sections introduce the reader to the model of graduate education that we use to illustrate the principles of structural modeling. The third section introduces the two components of structural modeling: the measurement model and the structural model. The remaining sections draw on a study of graduate student involvement in scholarly behavior (Nora, Cabrera, and Shinville, 1992) to show step by step how a structural model is used. We discuss methods available for assessing alternative models, indicators of goodness of fit, and procedures for testing the statistical significance of variables. Finally, we show how the results can be interpreted in practical terms.

New Directions for Institutional Research, no. 80, Winter 1993 © Jossey-Bass Publishers

41

Alternatives for Examining Graduate Education

Many methodological approaches can assist the researcher in the study of graduate education (Yancey, 1988). These statistical procedures range from the simple use of a one-way analysis of variance (ANOVA) to the more complex multivariate analysis of variance (MANOVA) and from simple hierarchical multiple regression to advanced structural modeling. The selection of one approach over another should be dictated by the nature of the research question under study and the dependent variable under consideration.

ANOVA and MANOVA are particularly appropriate when the question calls for comparisons across groups on a given set of educational outcomes (Marascuilo and Levin, 1983). For instance, Ethington and Pisani (1991) employed MANOVA to document the extent to which graduate education fostered development of professional skills and accomplishments across four categories of graduate students. Smart, Baird, and Bode (1991) used MANOVA to identify disciplinary learning demands associated with three doctoral programs. These two strategies are also pertinent when the researcher wants to document the net effects associated with a particular variable. Ethington and Pisani (1991) employed MANOVA to determine the net differences in graduate education outcomes across various groups of graduate students (for example, male and female, part time and full time) while removing the effect of job-related responsibilities that could have clouded the results of the investigation.

Logistic regression can be used to assess the overall effects when the outcome under consideration is dichotomous (Cabrera, in press; Fienberg, 1983; Hanusheck and Jackson, 1977). In such cases, no interval scales are accessible to describe the outcome under study. A graduate student is either engaged in research projects or not engaged. The student stays in the institution or leaves. The student does or does not obtain the doctoral degree. Cabrera (in press) relied on logistic regression to address the role of gains in conceptualizing skills on whether graduate students engage in scholarly behaviors.

However, when assessment focuses on exploring the underlying structural patterns embedded in the various factors associated with outcome measures of graduate programs, causal modeling is without doubt the most appropriate approach. Its techniques also allow the researcher to investigate indirect as well as direct effects of factors in final outcome measures of the graduate education process. Nora, Cabrera, and Shinville (1992) used causal modeling to determine the influence of pregraduate commitments, academic integration, departmental integration, and other factors on scholarly and professional engagement among doctoral students. This chapter draws on their model.

A Graduate Model of Attainment

Figure 4.1 shows the model of graduate education advanced by Nora, Cabrera, and Shinville (1992). The theoretical model presumes that occupational aspirations perceived to be associated with a particular graduate degree shape

Figure 4.1. Hypothesized Causal Model

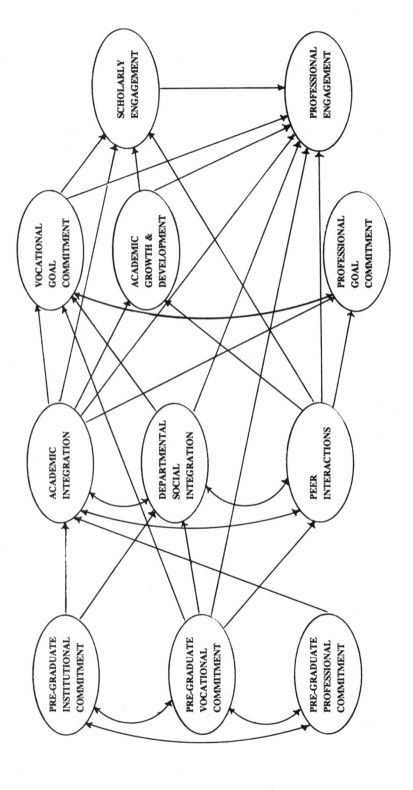

two types of predispositions (goals): attaining a graduate degree and selecting a particular institution (department and faculty). Predisposition toward securing a graduate degree are presumed to be associated with the individual's career aspirations and with the educational requirements associated with specific occupations. To the extent to which the individual perceives that a particular graduate school offers the desired graduate program, it is logical to expect the individual to regard the institution as instrumental in achieving his or her educational and career goals (Sewell and Hauser, 1980).

In accord with Clark's (1960) propositions, the model posits that these pregraduate school institutional and goal commitments embody values and attitudes toward graduate education that allow the individual to accept and conform to the demands, norms, and expectations imposed by the graduate department (Pascarella and Terenzini, 1991; Clark, 1960; Tinto, 1991)— acceptance and conformity that in turn make it possible for the graduate student to become integrated into the academic and social realms of the graduate department. The model further assumes that the student's integration is a dynamic process, that goal and institutional predispositions are affected by experiences and interactions with faculty and peers in the particular department, and that these experiences change or perhaps reinforce inclinations (commitments) on the part of the student to pursue vocational and/or academic and intellectual-oriented goals and commitments to remaining a member of a particular graduate department. A student's social and academic experiences in his or her department are likely to affect the student's goal aspirations. Moreover, the theoretical model also posits that the student is committed to the institution to the extent to which he or she perceives the department as instrumental in his or her attainment of the desired or valued outcomes.

The model posits that, as a consequence of interactions with the academic and social components of the department, the student experiences qualitative and quantitative changes that are reflected in the acquisition of graduate-level academic skills and abilities. These changes are manifested in the development of research skills and competencies at the graduate level. Finally, student gains reflected in acquiring the research skills necessary to engage in scholarly work subsequently affect the graduate student's involvement in behaviors (graduate-related outcomes) that are specific to graduate school (for example, presenting a research paper at a professional conference, doing research with a faculty member, attending meetings of professional organizations).

In sum, the structural model shown in Figure 4.1 asserts that measures of pregraduate institutional and goal commitments have direct effects on a graduate student's academic integration, social integration within the department, and peer group interactions. Academic Integration, Department Social Integration, Peer Interactions, and Pregraduate Vocational Commitment were hypothesized to have direct effects on measures of Vocational and Professional Goal Commitments, Academic Growth and Development, and direct and indirect effects on the two measures of scholarly behavior, Professional Engagement and Scholarly Engagement. Finally, Academic Growth and Development and the two measures of final commitment were hypothesized to have direct effects on the two outcome measures of scholarly involvement or behaviors (attendance at professional meetings and engaging in research). The model also reflects the noncausal relationships between integration factors, the three pre-graduate commitment factors, and the two final commitments.

The chapter uses information from a data base on graduate students at a major midwestern doctoral-granting institution to illustrate (Baird and Smart, 1991). Both part-time and full-time graduate students from all departments granting doctoral-level degrees were surveyed. A total of 711 doctoral graduate students was identified. These students received a mailed survey. Of this number, 603 responded, for an 85 percent response rate. Because data were missing on some key variables, the final usable sample consisted of 570 subjects.

We measured graduate students' commitments prior to enrollment in a doctoral program through preinstitutional commitment (two items), preprofessional commitment (one item), and prevocational commitment (a measure of the graduate student's initial commitment to attend graduate school related to vocational goals; two items). Academic contacts with faculty (a composite scale averaged across five items), intellectual development (composite scale; four items), and department commitment (composite scale; three items) provided indicators of a student's academic integration. Interactions with peers (a composite scale averaged across four items) provided a measure of a doctoral student's integration into the social component of the department in which he or she had enrolled. Final vocational commitment and final professional commitment were measured with a single item for each. Academic growth and development was measured via a conceptualizing skills scale (a composite averaged across six items) and a research skills scale (a composite averaged across four items). These scales measured the extent to which students reported that gains in conceptualization and research skills resulted from experiences with their respective academic departments. Membership in professional associations and attendance at professional meetings were used to measure professional engagement. Research engagement was measured through involvement in research and submission of research papers for publication.

Structural Modeling: Measurement and Structural Models

Structural modeling is not a statistical technique, nor is it a standardized set of routines that can be used to examine a specific research problem. Rather, structural modeling is a methodology or strategy that embraces both a measurement component and a structural component.

The Measurement Model. The measurement model portrays the pattern of measures for the constructs latent in the hypothesized causal model. It allows the researcher to test the soundness with which the variables in the quantitative model have been operationalized. The extent to which the measures reflect the constructs in the model is expressed in terms of loadings. A loading can also be viewed as an indicator of the extent to which the measure correlates with the factor or construct that it is supposed to measure. In addition to testing the hypothetical pattern of measures with their corresponding constructs, the measurement model can also be used to test the extent to which the constructs themselves overlap or are independent from one another. Independence is considered to be a test for the convergent and discriminant validity of the constructs under study (Anderson and Gerbing, 1988). In our example, that Academic Integration and Departmental Social Integration are independent constructs would be supported by the extent to which the measurement model indicates that the corresponding measures load significantly on the respective construct and that the amount of overlap between the two constructs is negligible.

Table 4.1 summarizes the measurement model that we used to develop indicators of the constructs in our structural model. We selected these measures after a series of confirmatory factor analyses indicated that they consti-

Table 4.1. Measurement Model

Construct Item or Scale	Number of Items	Cronbach Alpha	Loading	Unique Variance
Weighted Least Square Standardized Solution				
Professional Engagement	2	.691		
Membership in professional societies			.759	.423
Attendance at professional meetings			.986	.010
Scholarly Engagement	3	.804		
Research for meetings			.838	.298
Submission of papers			.987	.010
Publications			.891	.206
Academic Growth and Development				
Conceptualizing skills	6	.811	.902	.010
Research skills	4	.748	.593	.649
Academic Integration				
Intellectual development	4	.647	.689	.526
Contact with faculty	5	.848	.749	.200
Departmental commitment	3	.774	.719	.428
Peer Interactions	3	.627	.992	.010
Departmental Social Integration	1		.996	.010
Vocational Goal Commitment	1		.995	.010
Professional Goal Commitment	1		.995	.010
Pregraduate Institutional Commitment	2	.864	.992	.010
Pregraduate Vocational Commitment	2	.886	.987	.010
Pregraduate Professional Commitment	1		.996	.010

tuted the most reliable indicators of the corresponding constructs in the model. Factor loadings, unique variances, and modification indices were also estimated to ensure that measures for the indicators were valid before we tested the structural model.

The Structural Model. The second main component of structural modeling is the structural model itself. The structural model reflects the hypothesized relationships among constructs in the causal model through a series of structural equations. The structural equations reflect the direct and indirect effects among constructs that have been dictated by theory or suggested by research or personal experience. In this context, structural modeling is the process whereby presumed associations among latent (unobserved) constructs are submitted to empirical testing. As a function of the role that theory assigns to constructs in the model, a construct can be classified as endogenous or exogenous.

Exogenous constructs bring about a change in other constructs, and they are not influenced by other constructs in the model (Pedhazur, 1982). As Figure 4.1 shows, Pregraduate Institutional Commitment, Pregraduate Vocational Commitment, and Pregraduate Professional Commitment are exogenous constructs. The model makes no hypothesis about the constructs that can affect these pregraduate commitments.

Endogenous constructs are affected by exogenous constructs and other endogenous constructs in the causal model. In our study, Academic Integration, Departmental Social Integration, and Peer Interactions are endogenous variables. Note that all three also affect other constructs in the model.

In addition to displaying and estimating cause-and-effect relations, structural modeling can also help the institutional researcher to test for noncausal relationships among constructs as well as for reciprocal effects. Noncausal—also known as compensatory relationships—are relationships that reflect a degree of interrelation between latent constructs but that are not themselves of a causal nature. As Figure 4.1 shows, noncausal relationships can be found between Vocational Goal Commitment and Professional Goal Commitment and among the three exogenous latent constructs, namely Pregraduate Institutional Commitment, Pregraduate Vocational Commitment, and Pregraduate Professional Commitment.

In sum, the reason for modeling graduate education processes is to test the propositions advanced by the institutional researcher about how constructs are theoretically linked and the directionality of those relationships.

Assessing the Fit of a Model

In structural modeling, assessing the soundness of a particular model is carried out at two levels. At the first level, judgments assess the goodness or soundness of the overall causal model. At the second level, individual components of the model are evaluated. That is, the soundness of the propositions linking one construct with another is assessed.

Assessing Overall Fit of a Causal Model. The primary purpose of assessment at the first level is to determine the extent to which the hypothesized model as a whole plausibly represents the observed data. As Byrne (1989) has noted, the logic underlying the assessment of fit of a hypothesized model in structural modeling can be summarized with the following formula:

Data = Model + Residual

where *Data* represents the relationships observed among the variables under consideration, *Model* represents the network or relationships among constructs (illustrated in our case by Figure 4.1), and *Residual* refers to any difference between the hypothesized model and the observed data. When we test a model, we summarize these relationships in terms of either correlations or covariances. Assessing the validity of a hypothesized model requires us to judge how well the correlations or covariances associated with the hypothesized model actually reproduce the correlations or covariances observed. As an alternative, we can focus on the size of the discrepancy between the two. The smaller the residual, the more likely it is that the hypothesized model is a plausible representation of the reality reflected in the data.

Several indicators are available for assessing the goodness of fit of a given causal model. Some of the most commonly used and recommended are the chi-square statistic for overall fit, the goodness-of-fit index (GFI), the adjusted goodness-of-fit index (AGFI), the root mean square residual (RMR), the chi-square/degrees of freedom ratio, the adjusted normed fit index (NFI2), and the total coefficient of determination for the structural model. Bentler and Bonett (1980) discuss these and other indicators of fit. Other assessments and reviews of these indicators can be found in Marsh, Balla, and McDonald (1988) and in Mulaik, James, Van Alstine, Bennet, Lind, and Stillwell (1989).

Chi-Square Statistic. The chi-square statistic provides an overall indication of the discrepancy between the observed and the reproduced correlations or covariances (Bentler and Bonett, 1980). Contrary to the traditional interpretation of chi-square statistics, structural modeling judges the model to produce nonsignificant results when the p value associated with the chi-square is statistically significant. A statistically significant p value signifies that the hypothesized model departs significantly from the data. A nonsignificant p value indicates that there are no statistically significant differences between the observed correlations or covariances and those hypothesized by the model under consideration. In other words, the model appears to fit the data. As Table 4.2 shows, the p value associated with the chi-square for our study indicates that the graduate model failed to reproduce the observed data. However, we need to exercise caution when we use the chi-square value to judge the overall fit of a model. The chi-square is highly sensitive to sample size: As the sample size increases, the likelihood of rejecting the model also increases (Joreskog and Sorbom, 1989a, 1989b; Bentler and Bonett, 1980; Marsh, Balla, and McDonald, 1988). When n is very large, even trivial differences can lead

Table 4.2.   Overall Measures of Goodness of Fit
for a Causal Model

Goodness-of-Fit Measure	Statistical Value
Chi-square (df)	237.44(100)
Chi-square/degrees of freedom	2.37
Goodness-of-fit index	.984
Adjusted goodness-of-fit index	.975
Root mean square residual	.060
Normed fit index	.948
Total coefficient of determination	
for overall model	.320

to the rejection of a valid model (Bentler and Bonett, 1980). For this reason, Bentler and Bonett (1980) recommend that different measures of fit be taken into account simultaneously when the fit of a particular model is judged.

Chi-Square/Degrees of Freedom Ratio. The ratio of the chi-square to its degrees of freedom provides another indicator of how well the model fits the data. Since there are no known procedures for testing the statistical significance of this ratio, acceptable values have been suggested by Stage (1990), Carmines and McIver (1981), and Wheaton, Muthen, Alwin, and Summers (1977). Stage (1990) and Byrne (1989) recommend that a particular model be accepted whenever the value of the ratio is equal to or less than 2.5. Our model, which has a chi-square/degrees of freedom ratio of 2.37, meets this criterion.

Goodness-of-Fit Indexes. The goodness-of-fit index (GFI) and the adjusted goodness-of-fit index (AGFI) measure the relative amount of variance and covariance that are jointly accounted for by the model. The AGFI differs from the GFI by adjusting for the degrees of freedom in the model. The two measures range from 0 to 1, where values close to 1 indicate a good fit. For our model, the goodness-of-fit index was .984, and the adjusted goodness-of-fit index was .975. Both values indicate that the model fits the data.

The Root Mean Square Residual. The root mean square residual (RMR) represents a measure of the average residuals when the hypothesized correlation matrix is subtracted from the sample correlation matrix. Values less than .1 indicate that the model reproduced a sample correlation matrix closely resembling the underlying population correlation matrix. For our model, the root mean square residual was .06.

The Normed Fit Index. The normed fit index (NFI2), a technique advanced by Bentler and Bonett (1980) and improved on by Mulaik and others (1989), is another indicator of how well the model fits the data. Much in line with the chi-square, the NFI2 compares the fit of the model with the fit of an alternative model. Usually, the alternative model proposes that the relations observed among the variables were produced by chance. In other words, the alternative model presumes that no underlying factors account for the associations observed among the variables. To the extent to which the difference between the fit function of the hypothesized model and the fit function of the alternative model is large, the NFI2 approaches 1, signifying that the hypothesized causal model indeed represents a more plausible explanation as to how the variables are associated than the random assumption. The NFI2 for our model was .948.

The Total Coefficient of Determination. The total coefficient of determination for the overall hypothesized model represents the proportion of variance explained by the overall structural equations in the causal model. It is an indicator of how well the model as a whole explains the total variation associated with the data. The total coefficient of determination for the present model was .32 (32 percent). This index is analogous to the R^2 in multiple regression.

Summary. It is highly recommended that researchers not rely on any one indicator as a test of the significance of a model. An examination of the patterns of all seven measures of goodness-of-fit will provide a better indication of how well the model represents the data.

Assessing Individual Components of a Model. Beyond assessing the overall fit of the model, it is substantively important to assess the specific relations in the model. For example, Peer Interactions were hypothesized to influence Scholarly Engagement and Professional Engagement in the model; did the results support these hypothesized relationships? Figure 4.2 shows the results of the analyses and reveals that Peer Interaction was significantly related to Scholarly Engagement, but not to Professional Engagement. The following discussion of the results displayed in Figure 4.2 explains how to assess the significance of the relationships among the constructs in the model.

t-Values. These relationships are expressed in terms of structural coefficients (beta, gamma, phi, and psi coefficients). The sign associated with the structural weight indicates the direction of the effect that a particular variable has on the other variables. As Figure 4.2 shows, there is a significant positive direct effect from Academic Integration to Scholarly Engagement for our model. Various statistical solutions (for example, LISREL, EQS, LISCOMP, GEMINI) also estimate standard errors for each coefficient that the researcher can use to test the null hypothesis that a particular coefficient, such as Academic Integration, has no effect on one of the last endogenous (dependent) variables, such as Scholarly Engagement. The index used in covariance structure modeling for determining the statistical significance of individual structural coefficients is the *t*-value. This value is the ratio of the estimated parameter over its standard error. That is, the *t*-value equals $\beta_{academic\ integration}/SE_{academic\ integration}$. For our model, the *t*-value for the direct effect of Academic Integration on Scholarly Engagement was found to be significant at $p < .05$. *t*-values greater than 1.96 are considered to be statistically significant for a two-tailed test. However, most structural paths in causal models are based on theoretical premises that are specific as to the sign of the relationship, and values greater than 1.64 are therefore sufficient for a one-tailed test. Unless the researcher is uncertain whether

Figure 4.2. Full Structural Model

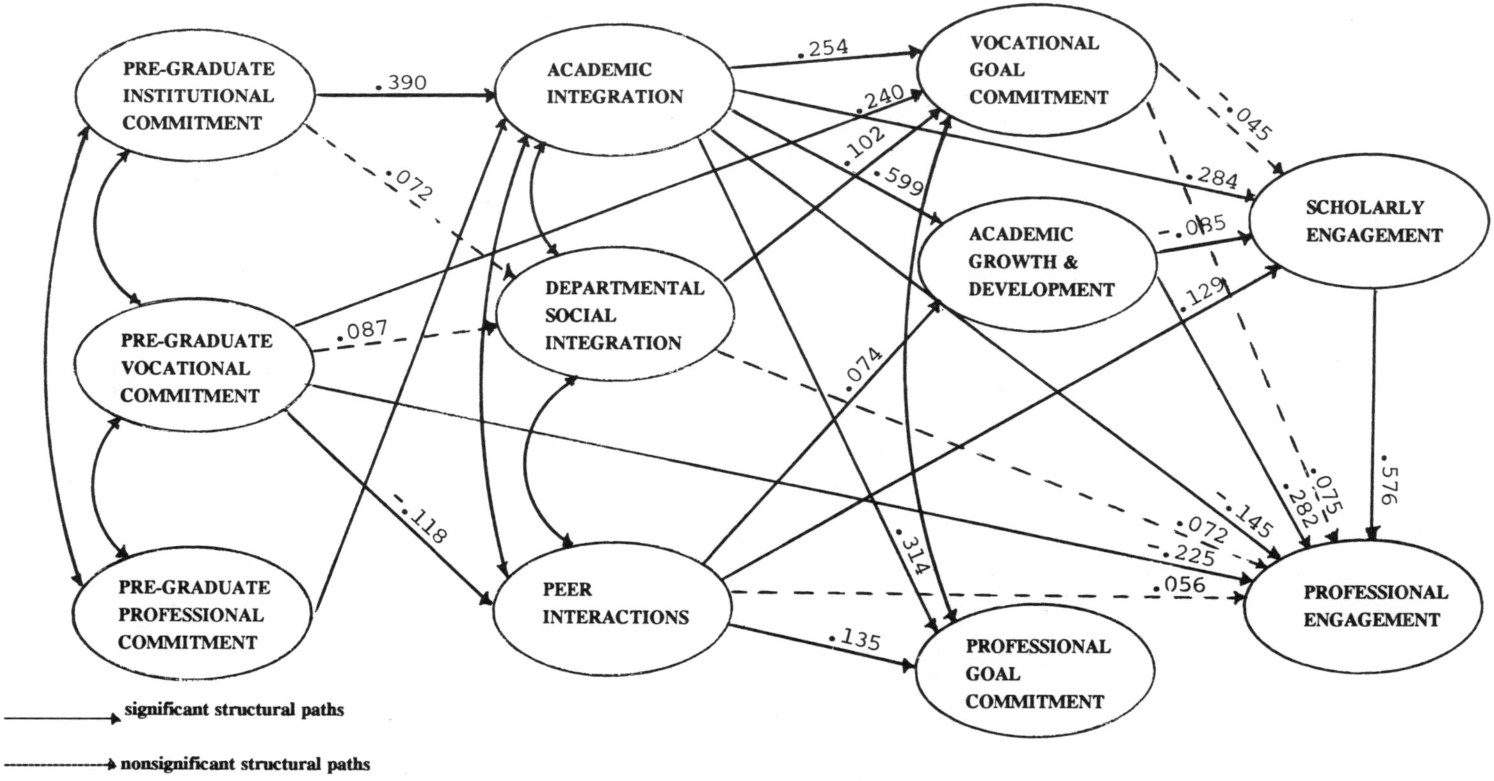

significant structural paths

nonsignificant structural paths

a variable has a negative or a positive effect on another variable, he or she should use a one-tailed test to determine statistical significance.

Coefficient of Determination. The overall causal model is composed of a set of structural equations. Each equation specifies the exogenous and endogenous variables that have been hypothesized to have a direct effect on individual endogenous (dependent) variables. A coefficient of determination (R^2) for the total set of equations in the model is produced, as discussed previously. But a separate R^2 is also derived for each structural equation in the model. Table 4.3 shows these equations and R^2 values. As in multiple regression analysis, the R^2 represents the total variance accounted for by the predictor variables in an equation. Our model hypothesized that Professional Engagement (one of eight dependent variables) was affected by five endogenous variables (Academic Integration, Departmental Social Integration, Peer Interactions, Academic Growth and Development, Vocational Goal Commitment) and one exogenous variable (Pregraduate Vocational Commitment). It was also related to the other criterion, Scholarly Engagement. The R^2 for Professional Engagement in the present study was .116. Thus, nearly 12 percent of the variance in Professional Engagement was explained by the six predictor variables in the equation.

Standardized Residuals and Q-Plot. For each parameter in the causal model that has been hypothesized, structural modeling estimates the discrepancy of fit between the sample and the hypothesized covariance matrices. Standard-

Table 4.3. Standardized Parameter Estimates (Weighted Least Square) for the Model

Independent Variables	Dependent Variables							
	AI	DI	PI	VGC	PGC	AGD	SCH ENG	PROF ENG
PGIC	.390*	.072						
PGVC		.087	−.118*	.240*				−.225*
PGPC	.181*							
AI				.254*	.314*	.599*	.284*	−.145*
DI				1.02				.072
PI					.135*	.074*	.129*	.056
VGC							−.045	.075
PGC								
AGD							−.085	.282*
SCHENG								.576*
PROFENG								
R^2	0.200	0.017	0.014	0.167	0.128	0.377	0.424	0.116

Notes: PGIC = Pregraduate Institutional Commitment; PGVC = Pregraduate Vocational Commitment; PGPC = Pregraduate Professional Commitment; AI = Academic Integration; DI = Departmental Social Integration; PI = Peer Interactions; VGC = Vocational Goal Commitment; PGC = Professional Goal Commitment; AGD = Academic Growth and Development; SCHENG = Scholarly Engagement; PROFENG = Professional Engagement. Asterisks indicate significant relations.

ized residuals, as opposed to residuals in their original metric, are analogous to Z-scores and represent estimates of the number of standard deviations of observed residuals from zero residuals that should exist if the causal model fits perfectly (Byrne, 1989). Standardized residuals that exceed ±2.00 for any element in the model are considered to represent model misspecification. For our model, the smallest standardized residual was -7.535, the largest standardized residual was 6.026, and the median for standardized residuals was .190. Only twenty-three of the hundred fifty-three standardized residuals in our model were found to exceed 2.0.

In conjunction with standardized residuals, structural modeling also provides a Q-plot. A Q-plot is a graphic representation of the residuals. Figure 4.3 shows the Q-plot for our model. Standardized residuals that follow the dotted line rising at a forty-five-degree angle in the Q-plot indicate a well-fitting model. Standardized residuals that deviate extremely from the forty-five-degree

Figure 4.3.   Q-Plot of Standardized Residuals

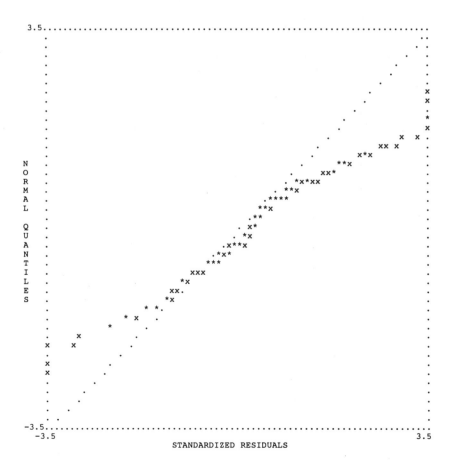

STANDARDIZED RESIDUALS

line in a nonlinear fashion indicate that the model is in some way misspecified (Byrne, 1989). An x in the Q-plot represents a single residual point and an asterisk represents multiple residual points (Joreskog and Sorbom, 1989a). For our data set, only a few standardized residuals were found to deviate. The small percentage of standardized residuals with values greater than 2.0 was evident in the Q-plot.

Modification Indexes. Structural modeling provides a modification index for each parameter in the hypothesized model that has been fixed at zero (for example, because it was not estimated) because of theoretical considerations. Modification indexes represent the expected drop in the chi-square value if a particular parameter is estimated or "freed" in the causal model. In other words, if the researcher respecified and reestimated the model, the decrease in the chi-square should at a minimum equal the value of the modification index, although it may be much larger. All parameters that have not been estimated in the quantitative model and that have modification indexes equal to or greater than 20 indicate the possibility of a relationship (Byrne, 1989). Byrne (1989, p. 57) cautions that the use of modification indexes must be based on theoretical considerations or possibilities: "If the researcher is unhappy with the overall fit of the hypothesized model, he or she can respecify a model in which this parameter is set free; the model is then reestimated. It must be emphasized, however, that the decision of whether or not to free this parameter must make substantive sense." It is recommended that parameters with modification indexes under 20 not be freed and reestimated because a significant drop in chi-square is unlikely and thus no significant improvement of fit will be made to the causal model under consideration. The maximum modification indexes for our model was 31.23. Although this value exceeds 20, we did not reestimate the model, because a respecification of the model would suggest that contact with academic faculty not only would provide a measure of Academic Integration for graduate students but would also load as an indicator of Professional Engagement. Because it does not make conceptual sense to respecify the model and because a significant drop in chi-square was not expected, we did not incorporate the loading suggested by the modification index into the final model. No other modification indexes had values exceeding 20.

Implications

The preceding sections, which were designed to give institutional researchers a basic understanding of structural modeling, advanced a model of graduate education grounded in theory and research. We introduced the institutional researcher to all indexes used in assessing the overall fit of the model and its individual components. To bring this chapter to a close, we will show how findings can help institutional researchers to assess or develop intervention strategies. We do not intend to fully elaborate on all the findings of our study.

All goodness-of-fit measures for our overall model indicate that it is empirically sound in validating the theoretical framework that we have proposed. Measures of both academic and social integration were significant in explaining scholarly behaviors as measured by involvement in professional meetings and research. Both factors not only contribute significantly in undergraduate studies but also directly affect scholarly and professional engagement in graduate education. While a negative causal relationship that was not hypothesized exists between Academic Integration and Professional Engagement (or the students' measured levels of involvement in professional organizations), it was negated by the large and significant positive indirect effect through intervening variables in the model.

Moreover, we found that students oriented toward occupational plans were less likely than graduate students oriented toward research to attend professional meetings and engage in research efforts either with fellow graduate students or with faculty, two very basic departmental goals of graduate programs. It appears that students whose sole purpose in attending graduate school is to earn a graduate degree for occupational advancement attach little value to involvement in professional organizations, and research associated with the student's field of study was also minimized.

Gains in conceptualization and research skills were not only found to have the largest effect on professional involvement, but indirectly they had an impact on the graduate student's research engagement. The results of our study indicate that the students who are academically and socially integrated into their respective departments in graduate school experience gains in their academic growth and development and subsequently become more involved in the scholarly behaviors specific to graduate education.

Our results further indicate that the socialization process in graduate school has a positive effect on gains made in conceptual and research skills and on research involvement. Students who are more actively involved in forming relationships with peers for the purpose either of socializing or of discussing academic topics are more likely to develop positive attitudes toward acquiring the skills needed in graduate school to engage in research. These results are consistent with departmental goals at the institution under study of encouraging graduate students to interact to enhance intellectual curiosity and exchange knowledge and ideas.

If the focus of intervention is to increase the involvement of graduate students in research or in professional organizations, the results suggest specific areas that intervention strategists may consider. The model implies that changes in participation in scholarly engagement can be brought about by programs that address the academic and social integration of graduate students. Faculty development workshops focusing on the mentoring relationship between graduate student and faculty member are one mechanism for increasing the contact between them and thus in promoting the student's academic integration. Giving students opportunities to interact within their departments may help to facilitate the social integration of graduate students. Changes in the curriculum that require graduate students to develop research papers for submission to professional organizations may enhance students' participation in professional conferences. Such a requirement would increase the likelihood that a graduate student would experience growth in conceptual and research skills, a factor found to exert a positive effect on professional engagement. The two intervention strategies just outlined exemplify some avenues available to the institutional researcher. This is not an exhaustive listing of possible intervention activities specific to research findings. We offer the preceding as examples of intervention strategies that the institutional researcher can consider once he or she has been able to untangle and estimate the relative importance of factors in the graduate education process. In sum, a universe of strategies can be considered once these factors and their interrelationships have been determined. Structural modeling serves the purpose of uncovering and identifying the interrelations among factors that can guide intervention strategies.

Concluding Remarks

Because graduate education has been the object of little research, causal modeling remains a powerful alternative for institutional researchers as a means of discovering interrelations among the factors that inform graduate education processes. However, the effectiveness with which causal modeling can be used is highly dependent on its systematic and careful application. Throughout this chapter, we have suggested that the conceptualization of structural models should be predicated on sound theoretical propositions. Theoretical frameworks, extant research, and personal experience can all help to select variables to be used in causal modeling and to formulate propositions on how the constructs are interrelated. Moreover, structural modeling can help the researcher to select the scales or items that are the most reliable and valid indicators for the constructs under consideration. Finally, both the measurement and the structural models can be submitted to empirical investigation. Several indicators of fit have been discussed that can help an institutional researcher to determine the soundness of the hypothesized causal model and its components. Although the process of model testing may be cumbersome, time-consuming, and demanding, the payoff is substantial when we note that the knowledge acquired can help to focus intervention strategists on key variables and their interrelationships.

References

Anderson, J. C., and Gerbing, D. W. "Structural Equation Modeling in Practice: A Review and Recommended Two-Step Approach." *Psychological Bulletin,* 1988, *103,* 411–423.

Baird, L. L., and Smart, J. C. "Graduate Students and Their Academic and Professional Development: A Study of Interactions Among Personal Characteristics, Life Circumstances, and Graduate School Experiences." Paper presented at the annual meeting of the Association for the Study of Higher Education, Boston, November 1991.

Bentler, P. M. "Multivariate Analysis with Latent Variables: Causal Modeling." *Annual Review of Psychology,* 1980, *31,* 419–456.

Bentler, P. M. *EQS: Structural Equations Program Manual.* Los Angeles: BMDP Software, 1989.

Bentler, P. M., and Bonett, D. G. "Significance Tests and Goodness of Fit in the Analysis of Covariance Structures." *Psychological Bulletin*, 1980, *88*, 586–606.

Byrne, B. M. *A Primer of LISREL: Basic Applications and Programming for Confirmatory Factor Analytic Models*. New York: Springer-Verlag, 1989.

Cabrera, A. F. "Logistic Regression Analysis in Higher Education: An Applied Perspective." In J. C. Smart (ed.), *Higher Education: Handbook of Theory and Research*. Vol. 10. New York: Agathon Press, in press.

Carmines, E. G., and McIver, S. P. "Analyzing Models with Unobserved Variables: Analysis of Covariance Structures." In G. W. Bohrnstedt and E. F. Borgatta (eds.), *Social Measurement: Current Issues*. Newbury Park, Calif.: Sage, 1981.

Clark, B. "The 'Cooling-Out' Function in Higher Education." *American Journal of Sociology*, 1960, *65*, 569–576.

Ethington, C. A., and Pisani, A. "The RA and TA Experience: Impediments and Benefits to Graduate Study." Paper presented at the annual meeting of the Association for the Study of Higher Education, Boston, Nov. 1991.

Fienberg, S. E. *The Analysis of Cross-Classified Categorical Data*. (rev. ed.) Cambridge: Massachusetts Institute of Technology, 1983.

Hanusheck, E. K., and Jackson, J. E. *Statistical Methods for Social Scientists*. San Diego, Calif.: Academic Press, 1977.

Joreskog, K. G., and Sorbom, D. *LISREL VII*. Mooresville, Ind.: Scientific Software, 1989a.

Joreskog, K. G., and Sorbom, D. *PRELIS: A Program for Multivariate Data Screening and Data Summarization—A Preprocessor for LISREL*. Mooresville, Ind.: Scientific Software, 1989b.

Marascuilo, L. A., and Levin, J. R. *Multivariate Statistics in the Social Sciences: A Researcher's Guide*. Monterey, Calif.: Brooks/Cole, 1983.

Marsh, H. W., Balla, J. R., and McDonald, R. P. "Goodness-of-Fit Indexes in Confirmatory Factor Analysis: The Effect of Sample Size." *Psychological Bulletin*, 1988, *103* (3), 391–410.

Mulaik, S. A., James, L. R., Van Alstine, J., Bennett, N., Lind, S., and Stillwell, C. D. "Evaluation of Goodness-of-Fit Indices for Structural Equation Models." *Psychological Bulletin*, 1989, *105*, 430–445.

Muthen, B. O. *LISCOMP: Analysis of Linear Structural Equations with a Comprehensive Measurement Model*. Mooresville, Ind.: Scientific Software, 1988.

Nora, A., Cabrera, A. F., and Shinville, P. "Graduate Student Involvement in Scholarly Behavior: A Structural Model." Paper presented at the annual meeting of the American Educational Research Association, San Francisco, Apr. 1992.

Pascarella, E. T., and Terenzini, P. T. *How College Affects Students: Findings and Insights from Twenty Years of Research*. San Francisco: Jossey-Bass, 1991.

Pedhazur, E. J. *Multiple Regression in Behavioral Research: Explanation and Prediction*. San Francisco: Jossey-Bass, 1982.

Sewell, W., and Hauser, R. "The Wisconsin Longitudinal Study of Social and Psychological Factors in Aspirations and Achievements." In A. Kerckhoff (ed.), *Research in the Sociology of Education and Socialization*. Greenwich, Conn.: JAI Press, 1980.

Smart, J. C., Baird, L. L., and Bode, R. "Discipline Differences in the Learning Demands of Doctoral Programs." Paper presented at the annual meeting of the Association for the Study of Higher Education, Boston, Nov. 1991.

Stage, F. "LISREL: An Introduction and Application in Higher Education." In J. C. Smart (ed.), *Higher Education: Handbook of Theory and Research*. Vol. 6. New York: Agathon Press, 1990.

Tinto, V. "Toward a Theory of Doctoral Persistence." Paper presented at the annual meeting of the American Educational Research Association, Chicago, Apr. 1991.

Wheaton, B., Muthen, B., Alwin, D. F., and Summers, G. F. "Assessing Reliability and Stability in Panel Models." In D. R. Heise (ed.), *Sociological Methodology*, 1977. San Francisco: Jossey-Bass, 1977.

Yancey, B. D. (ed.). *Applying Statistics in Institutional Research*. New Directions for Institutional Research, no. 58. San Francisco: Jossey-Bass, 1988.

AMAURY NORA is associate professor in the College of Education at the University of Illinois, Chicago.

ALBERTO F. CABRERA is assistant professor in the Department of Educational Administration and Policy Studies at the School of Education, State University of New York, Albany.

Since 1958, the National Research Council has gathered information on doctoral recipients. This information, which is available annually in data tape form to supplying institutions, gives these institutions an opportunity to improve their understanding of their doctoral recipients.

The Use of Retrospective National Data for Institutional Evaluation

James Ploskonka

The time required for college and university students to complete the doctoral process has recently become a major concern for university officials (Blum, 1992; Evangelauf, 1988). The anticipation of severe faculty shortages primarily in the humanities and social sciences has further heightened the concern of higher education specialists (Bowen and Sosa, 1989). In virtually every area of study, graduate students are taking longer to complete their degree requirement than at any other point in the recorded history of American higher education. In view of the unacceptable and continuing trend toward lengthening time to doctoral completion, the shortages in faculty expected at all levels, and the relatively small number of empirical studies addressing this issue, it is both timely and necessary to research the factors that affect time to the doctorate (Bowen and Rudenstine, 1992).

For .6 percent of the United States population, completion of the doctoral degree marks the pinnacle of the American formal educational process (Brazziel and Beeler, 1991). Completion has been described as a socialization process to an authoritative professional position (Baird, 1990). The amount of energy, time, personal resources, and financial resources involved in this arduous process has been studied to varying degrees. The beginning of the process—the undergraduate experience—has received the most attention from researchers (Pascarella and Terenzini, 1991). However, the graduate portion of the process has been the subject of relatively few studies since 1976 (Malaney, 1988). Nevertheless, interest in this area has recently increased. One can speculate that this increase is related to concern about the future of the work force, especially in terms of supply and demand for professors. Another reason might be the demographic changes now being observed on American campuses.

NEW DIRECTIONS FOR INSTITUTIONAL RESEARCH, no. 80, Winter 1993 © Jossey-Bass Publishers

Bernard Berelson (1960) conducted the first comprehensive study of grad uate education in the United States slightly more than thirty years ago. The subsequent literature on the amount of time elapsed between completion of the baccalaureate and receipt of the doctorate is moderate (Tuckman, Coyle, and Bae, 1990; Tinto, 1991; Bowen and Sosa, 1989; Ott, Markewich, and Ochsner, 1984), yet concern over anticipated shortages of college professors, researchers, and so on expressed by higher education specialists, external agencies, and governmental officials (Nerad, 1990; Berger, 1989) underscores the importance of investigating the factors related to completion of the doc torate (Baird, 1990). Table 5.1 shows median years to the doctorate between 1960 and 1989. The increase in both registered time (which includes part-time and full-time status at the graduate level) and total time (registered plus non-registered status at the graduate level) suggests that these concerns are well motivated.

Factors Affecting Time to the Doctorate

The positive representation of graduate education in the United States, reflected by increases in the number of doctoral-granting institutions and the types of students and programs involved may paint a positive picture of the development of graduate education in the United States. Nevertheless, the increasing time of doctoral study from 8.5 to 10.5 median years between 1958 and 1989 has higher education specialists concerned (Tuckman, Coyle, and Bae, 1990; Evangelauf, 1989).

This development has negative implications for American colleges and universities. If students are discouraged from the quest for a doctorate because of the amount of time needed to fulfill the requirements for completion (Tuckman, Coyle, and Bae, 1990), then the negative implications are not just for the students but for society as well: "There is a particularly strong national stake in graduate education. Talented and highly motivated graduate students—both as students and later as faculty members—contribute to our collective capacity to generate new ideas as well as to educate new generations of students. In these ways, they add immeasurably to the intellectual capital of the country. Graduate education benefits the society as a whole, not just individual students; it is essential to our ability as a nation to achieve political, social and moral objectives, as well as economic and technological progress.

Table 5.1.   Median Years to Doctoral Degree

	1960	1965	1969	1973	1977	1983	1985	1989
Registered	5.3	5.5	5.5	5.8	6.1	6.4	6.8	6.9
Total	8.8	8.2	8.0	8.4	8.7	9.4	10.2	10.5

Source: Turgood and Weinman, 1990, p. 16.

In important respects, it is the foundation of higher learning on which so much else depends" (Bowen and Sosa, 1990, p. 172).

This chapter shows how individual institutions can make use of national data tapes to address concerns and answer questions. Every year, the National Research Council (NRC) makes the Doctorate Records File available free of charge to institutions that submit completed copies of the Survey of Earned Doctorates to it. Since 1958, the NRC's Office of Scientific and Engineering Personnel or one of its forerunner organizations has collected and distributed data based on this retrospective questionnaire with the cooperation of graduate deans of accredited United States universities. Doctoral graduates complete the instrument at the time when they complete all requirements for the doctoral degree. The graduate dean's office forwards completed questionnaires to the NRC, which is located in Washington, D.C. The NRC annually presents the resulting data in aggregate form, for example, *Summary Report 1989: Doctorate Recipients from United States Universities* (Turgood and Weinman, 1990). This survey gathers information related to the personal background characteristics of doctoral recipients (for example, place and date of birth, national origin, parent's highest level of education, handicapped status, race, sex, number of dependents, and marital status), prior education and interests, source of financial support, and debt accumulated. The questionnaire also asks for information related to postdoctoral plans. The information obtained in the survey has been transformed and enhanced since 1958 to clarify the description of doctoral recipients (Turgood and Weinman, 1990).

Between 1920 and 1957, the tape documentation for the Doctorate Records File was compiled from information collected and submitted by degree-granting institutions (commencement bulletins, student files, and so forth). Although the information for early years is limited to the doctoral recipient's name; sex; baccalaureate and master's institution and year of completion; and doctoral institution, discipline, and year of completion, it provides a base not readily available to institutions who have not developed or maintained such records.

The NRC data set includes a wide variety of qualitative and quantitative variables that permit an institution to describe doctoral recipients without altering the data. Moreover, the NRC data tapes permit an institution to compare its doctoral recipients with the national cohort of doctoral recipients through supplemental publications of the National Research Council.

To illustrate the kinds of analysis that can be conducted, this chapter focuses on a data set obtained from a large public Carnegie Research I university (Carnegie Foundation for the Advancement of Teaching, 1987) representing 3,787 doctoral recipients between 1929 and 1989. I used this data set for my doctoral dissertation (Ploskonka, 1992). The institution had not used the corresponding data tape. Its only other source for similar data is individual student folders, most of which are housed in the university's archives.

The variables contained in the data set are organized into five major sections. Personal background characteristics are traditional demographic measures. They comprise ten variables, age, number of dependents, place of birth, sex, marital status, citizenship, handicapped status, parent's education level, and racial and ethnic affiliation. The section devoted to prior education and interests permits the researcher to identify where doctoral recipients came from academically and when. The variables included in this section include state or country of high school, year of high school graduation, junior college attendance, state or country of first college, year of college entrance, institution of first baccalaureate or equivalent, major field of baccalaureate, year of baccalaureate, year of entrance to graduate school, institution of first master's or equivalent degree, major field of first master's or professional degree, year of first master's degree, type of professional doctorate, doctorate institution, major field of doctorate, field of dissertation, calendar year and month of all degrees earned, type of doctorate, time not enrolled in a college or university, total time enrolled, and enrollment status. The information on enrollment status includes number of years as a full-time student, number of years as a part-time student, and number of years not enrolled.

The section on financial aid and support has been of particular interest nationally. Fortunately, this portion of the data set provides information on the following variables: sources of primary and secondary support, cumulative debt, and predoctoral employment status. Another section, postdoctoral aspirations and opportunities, permits the researcher to determine the postdoctoral employment or research intentions of doctoral recipients. The variables in this section are postdoctoral status or plans, postdoctoral field of study, postdoctoral source of support, postdoctoral employment and type of employer, primary work activity, postdoctoral employment field, decision against postdoctoral study, institution and/or place of postdoctoral affiliation.

I added a numeric code for the chair of the dissertation committee so I could conduct a statistical analysis of the impact of the chair on time to the degree. In addition to the description of departments or major field of studies, the ratio of dissertation chair to doctoral recipients can be expressed. The dissertation chair variable was taken directly from the recipient's folder within a specified period of time. Another option for augmenting the national data set is to obtain current data tapes at the institution or national level from an organization like Educational Testing Service and merge the data by social security number. For example, the Educational Testing Service will supply an institution with a tape containing Graduate Record Examination scores for individuals who selected the institution. This alternative is preferable to extracting information from individual folders.

Empirical studies on time to completion demonstrate that age (Tuckman, Coyle, and Bae, 1990), sex (Teague-Rice, 1981; Benkin, 1983), race (Vaughn, 1985), and number of dependents and citizenship (Abedi and Benkin, 1987) are related to the length of doctoral study. Changing institutions between completion of the bachelor's and doctoral degrees (Nerad and Cerny, 1991), working outside the university environment (Wilson, 1965), quality of the program

(Solomon, 1976), departmental differences (Baird, 1990), and career goals (Tuckman, Coyle, and Bae, 1990) have also been shown to affect the duration of doctoral study.

Table 5.2 shows how the NRC data set can be used for the purposes of institutional assessment. *Research I* and *Comprehensive I* represent Carnegie Research University I and Comprehensive College or University I classifications. As Table 5.2 shows, a great deal of information can be extracted from the national data source, which limits the time required of the researcher. Moreover, in view of the variables listed, such regression techniques as multivariate analysis and event history analysis (Willett and Singer, 1991; Allison, 1984) can be applied. Use of time measures of doctoral studies as dependent variables can give decision makers the information they need about the influences on time to the doctorate.

Another strategy is to chart trends in various variables over time. For example, the ten- or twenty-year trends in proportion of doctorates awarded to women, minority students, and students in various fields of study and specialization could be studied. Trends in financial support, postdoctoral plans, and type of undergraduate institution could be studied in a similar way. And, of course, trends in various time-to-degree measures could also be examined.

Still another strategy is to compare time to degree with recipients' standing on other variables, such as type of financial support (for example, research assistantship, teaching assistantship, college loan), change in discipline of study, and receipt of a master's as a prerequisite for the doctorate. All these analyses would show the effects of various conditions on time to the doctorate. These analyses can be very informative. They are easy to conduct once the institutional researcher is familiar with the data set.

Regression analysis of these data sets can also be used to predict time to the doctorate. For example, statistical analysis of variables predicting time to the doctorate at the university that I studied confirms the finding of previous studies (Abedi and Benkin, 1987; Gillingham, Seneca, and Taussig, 1991) that the strongest predictor of time to the doctorate at all transition time points was primary source of support. However, in contrast to Abedi and Benkin (1987), I did not find that number of dependents influenced time to the degree when I included marital status in the regression equation. Moreover, sex was unrelated to total time from college entrance—a finding consistent with the research on doctoral recipients at the University of California at Los Angeles (Abedi and Benkin, 1987).

Field of study was found to be predictive for total time periods but not for registered time periods when other variables were controlled for. Variance decomposition was then used to explore the differences between nested groups within the field of study variable. Area of specialization accounted for a smaller portion of the variance than field of study but a larger portion than dissertation chair in all the transition time points. I was not able to demonstrate that the dissertation chair affects time to the doctoral degree as Nerad (1990), Dickerson (1987), and Benkin (1984) have suggested.

Table 5.2. Doctoral Recipients Compared by Field of Study

Variables	Agriculture	Biological Sciences	Education	Engineering	Health	Humanities	Mathematics	Physical Sciences	Professional	Psychology	Social Sciences
Mean Age at Doctorate	31.92	31.20	39.32	31.57	30.97	35.96	32.07	31.15	35.91	33.28	34.92
Percentage Male	89.78	79.07	66.28	98.96	84.00	64.77	88.11	90.85	85.71	72.09	83.91
Percentage Female	10.22	20.93	33.72	1.04	16.00	35.23	11.90	9.15	14.29	29.31	16.09
Percentage Married	75.92	72.05	78.33	65.75	77.14	68.02	70.92	74.47	81.25	70.69	75.68
Mean Number of Dependents	1.25	1.11	1.43	1.34	1.16	1.33	1.55	1.01	1.58	1.25	1.43
Percentage White	79.12	81.58	90.35	49.35	70.15	91.46	86.84	78.57	85.53	95.19	82.84
Percentage African American	4.03	1.88	5.63	1.95	2.99	2.49	1.32	0.00	1.89	1.92	3.73
Percentage Asian/Pacific Islander	15.02	13.91	2.14	45.45	25.37	1.42	9.21	19.29	11.32	1.44	13.06
Percentage BS Same Field	68.83	61.76	33.28	76.68	61.33	75.32	67.86	73.48	62.64	58.01	53.56
Percentage Research I Universities	49.10	35.00	32.00	64.30	66.70	25.00	9.50	25.60	24.20	44.60	37.00
Percentage Comprehensive I Universities	14.30	22.80	28.00	14.30	6.70	26.10	25.80	41.00	37.90	20.80	27.20
Percentage MS Same Field	74.56	48.32	62.02	83.94	26.67	77.22	70.83	49.70	89.71	66.75	66.53

Primary Source of Support											
Percentage Family/Personal	13.23	17.33	70.39	13.26	9.52	33.53	17.65	15.73	53.16	44.59	25.32
Percentage Teaching Assistantship	0.53	17.88	6.87	10.20	33.33	1.83	58.82	33.71	22.52	21.62	32.28
Percentage Research Assistantship	67.20	42.46	7.30	56.12	19.05	45.73	13.73	22.47	5.41	10.14	11.39
Percentage Fellowship	2.12	8.38	2.15	8.16	4.76	0.61	3.92	5.62	1.80	4.05	3.80
Parent's Educational Level											
Father: High School or Less	60.97	48.38	65.46	46.55	60.61	51.61	51.19	59.00	56.06	48.47	56.67
Father: At Least Some College	39.03	51.62	34.54	53.45	39.39	48.39	48.81	41.00	43.94	51.53	43.33
Mother: High School or Less	66.86	64.89	64.82	63.98	82.82	55.11	54.34	65.00	68.84	62.12	61.80
Mother: At Least Some College	33.14	35.11	35.18	36.02	17.18	44.89	45.66	35.00	31.16	37.88	38.20
Mean Total Time from College Entrance	13.37	12.87	20.55	13.61	12.86	17.84	13.54	13.08	17.05	14.75	16.15
Mean Registered Time from College Entrance	10.48	10.31	12.41	10.41	10.03	13.18	11.00	11.21	10.93	11.85	11.54
Mean Total Time from Graduate Entrance	7.69	7.38	13.36	6.97	6.31	11.77	8.54	7.92	10.97	9.40	10.05
Mean Registered Time from Graduate Entrance	6.32	6.26	8.30	5.74	5.50	9.00	7.07	7.03	6.73	7.77	7.46

Note: Statistics are based on the number of recipients in a field.

Interpreting the Results

The results of analysis have implications for policies and practice that need to be explored. The results for the institution that I examined suggested some general areas that warranted further investigations. The limited number of minorities may suggest that the institution is not supportive of minorities seeking the doctorate. However, the distribution of minorities varies by field of study, from which we can infer that the chosen academic discipline may hinder the process for persons of color. Additional data and research are required if we are to assess the direct and indirect effects on minority students. The reasons that Vaughn (1985) cited for the longer times that minorities take to complete the doctoral degree—poverty, unemployment, lack of ethnically similar mentors—were beyond the scope of my study, but the area warrants further exploration.

The glaring differences in the distribution of female and male doctoral recipients demonstrate that women do not receive advanced degrees in the same numbers as men. Some fields of study have produced a greater percentage of females than other fields, but the distribution in all fields is not comparable to males. Moreover, the distribution of financial resources by the institution, which focuses its resources in certain fields—agriculture, mathematics, engineering—potentially limits the primary financial support awarded to women, since women are not concentrated in these fields. The resulting disparity extends the doctoral process. Does the structure of the distribution of institutional resources indirectly favor male over female doctoral students? Does the institution need to make additional monies available to reduce time to the doctorate?

As part of the process to determine length of time to the degree, researchers should be clear about time of doctoral entrance, and they need to distinguish between students who complete a master's degree before undertaking the doctoral degree and students who do not. In my study (Ploskonka, 1992) and in those of Bowen and Rudenstine (1992), Wilson (1965), and Berelson (1960), the time at which a person enters the doctoral process is masked by the time at which he or she enters graduate school. As I have shown, time not enrolled is greatest between academic transition points, one of which is the period between completion of the master's degree and commencement of doctoral studies.

In addition to quantitative studies, qualitative research techniques should be used to observe doctoral students in pursuit of the degree. Analysis of the ways in which frustration, motivation, and so on influence time to the doctoral degree would be particularly interesting. Institutional programs that are designed to assist students, such as housing and child care (Nerad, 1991), should be emphasized. Individual motivation, another variable that may be a major predictor of time to completion, should also be studied.

Since my study was limited to a single institution, readers should be cautious about generalizing my findings to other institutions of higher learning.

Supplementary research in this area should include data from a variety of institutions along Carnegie classification types and geographical locations. The study by Bowen and Rudenstine (1992) is an excellent example of the ways in which similar institutions can be compared. Their work is a model for efforts to compare an assortment of types of institutions from varying geographical areas. Such analyses would enlarge our view of the pursuit of the doctoral degree.

Thirty-three years ago, Bernard Berelson (1960) emphasized the importance of monitoring the duration of the doctorate. Today, the question, at both the local and national levels (Bowen and Rudenstine, 1992), centers on the reduction of time to the doctorate. My study explored the length of time it took graduate students at a large public Carnegie Research I university to complete the doctoral degree process. With NRC data tapes, I produced a description and profile of the population.

The example explored in this chapter shows institutional researchers how they can develop information that faculty, administrators, and external agencies can use in their efforts to enhance and study the graduate education process. Further exploration will offer insight into the factors that an institution or student may be able to influence. Such insight should help students to complete their programs in an efficient and timely manner.

References

Abedi, J., and Benkin, E. M. "The Effects of Students' Academic, Financial, and Demographic Variables on Time to the Doctorate." *Research in Higher Education,* 1987, *27,* 3–14.

Allison, P. D. *Event History Analysis: Regression for Longitudinal Event Data.* Newbury Park, Calif.: Sage, 1984.

Baird, L. L. "The Melancholy of Anatomy: The Personal and Professional Development of Graduate and Professional School Students." In J. C. Smart (ed.), *Higher Education: Handbook of Theory and Research.* Vol. 6. New York: Agathon Press, 1990.

Benkin, E. M. "Where Have All the Doctoral Students Gone: A Study of Doctoral Attrition at U.C.L.A." Unpublished doctoral dissertation, College of Education, University of California, Los Angeles, 1984.

Berelson, B. *Graduate Education in the United States.* New York: McGraw-Hill, 1960.

Berger, J. "Slow Pace Toward Doctorate Prompts Fear of Unfilled Jobs." *New York Times,* May 3, 1989, p. 1.

Blum, D. E. "Attrition of Ph.D. Candidates and the Time Spent Earning Degree Called Unacceptable." *Chronicle of Higher Education,* Jan. 29, 1992, pp. A33–A34.

Bowen, W. G., and Rudenstine, N. L. *In Pursuit of the Ph.D.* Princeton, N.J.: Princeton University Press, 1992.

Bowen, W. G., and Sosa, J. A. *Prospects for Faculty in the Arts and Sciences.* Princeton, N.J.: Princeton University Press, 1989.

Brazziel, W. F., and Beeler, K. J. "Doctorate Production and a Changing Demography." Paper presented at the annual meeting of the Association for the Study of Higher Education, Boston, Oct. 1991.

Carnegie Foundation for the Advancement of Teaching. *A Classification of Institutions of Higher Education.* Princeton, N.J.: Carnegie Foundation for the Advancement of Teaching, 1987.

Dickerson, D. "Doctoral Programs Said to Share Blame When Students Fail to Complete Theses." *Chronicle of Higher Education,* July 17, 1987, p. 31.

Evangelauf, J. "Lengthening of Time to Earn a Doctorate Causes Concern." *Chronicle of Higher Education,* March 15, 1989, p. 13.

Gillingham, L., Seneca, J. J., and Taussig, M. K. "The Determinants of Progress to the Doctoral Degree." *Research in Higher Education,* 1991, *32,* 449–468.

Malaney, G. "Graduate Education as an Area of Research in Higher Education." In J. C. Smart (ed.), *Higher Education: Handbook of Theory and Research.* Vol. 4. New York: Agathon Press, 1988.

Nerad, M. *Factors Affecting Completion of Doctoral Degrees at the University of California: A Report Prepared in Response to Senate Concurrent Resolution 66 (Hart, 1989).* Oakland: University of California, 1990.

Nerad, M., and Cerny, J. "From Facts to Action: Expanding the Educational Role of the Graduate Division." *Communicator,* May 1991, pp. 1–13.

Ott, M., Markewich, T., and Ochsner, N. "Logit Analysis of Graduate Student Retention." *Research in Higher Education,* 1984, *21,* 439–459.

Pascarella, E. T., and Terenzini, P. T. *How College Affects Students: Findings and Insights from Twenty Years of Research.* San Francisco: Jossey-Bass, 1991.

Ploskonka, J. "An Exploratory Model of Doctoral Completion: A Description of Characteristics and Their Relationship to Time to the Degree." Unpublished doctoral dissertation, College of Education, University of Kentucky, 1992.

Solomon, L. C. *Male and Female Graduate Students.* New York: Praeger, 1976.

Teague-Rice, L. "A Profile of the Female Doctoral Student Who Persisted to the Completion of the Doctoral Degree." Unpublished doctoral dissertation, Department of Education, Auburn University, 1981.

Tinto, V. "Toward a Theory of Doctoral Persistence." Paper presented at the annual meeting of the American Educational Research Association, Chicago, Apr. 1991.

Tuckman, H., Coyle, S., and Bae, Y. *On Time to the Doctorate.* Washington, D.C.: National Academy Press, 1990.

Turgood, D. H., and Weinman, J. M. *Summary Report 1989: Doctorate Recipients from United States Universities.* Washington, D.C.: National Academy Press, 1990.

Vaughn, J. C. "Minority Students in Graduate Education." In B. L. Smith (ed.), *The State of Graduate Education.* Washington, D.C.: Brookings Institutions, 1985.

Willett, J. B., and Singer, J. D. "How Long Did it Take? Using Survival Analysis in Educational and Psychological Research." In L. M. Collins and J. L. Hart (eds.), *Best Methods for the Analysis of Change: Research Advances, Unanswered Questions, Future Directions.* Washington, D.C.: American Psychological Association, 1991.

Wilson, K. M. *Of Time and the Doctorate: Report of and Inquiry into the Duration of Doctoral Study.* Atlanta, Ga.: Southern Regional Education Board, 1965.

JAMES PLOSKONKA is associate director for residence life at the University of Kentucky, Lexington.

*A framework is presented for considering changes in graduate educa-
tion that will help decrease student frustration. Policy changes are
linked to practical considerations.*

Enhancing Success in Doctoral
Education: From Policy to Practice

Susan S. Lipschutz

When a creative writing student at the University of Tulsa was asked to com-
ment on a drawing of an artifact from a mythical culture, she described the
drawing as "a scroll from . . . a country whose language and expression were
musical, in our terms, and yet mute. . . . The scroll, though old, is not scarred
by time but rather by a 'machine' which played the language. . . . One can tell
which ideas were most dear to these people; truth is badly worn" (Beach, 1992,
p. B36).

   One can also read the truth about certain aspects of graduate education
in the candid reflections of graduate degree holders—and of those who never
received their degree. There, too, we find truths so obvious that they are badly
worn. While many happy and productive faculty members may remember
their graduate work with gratitude and nostalgia, for many others—those who
hold the degree as well as those who do not—graduate school represented
years of frustration and self-doubt. In particular, combining the residue of bit-
terness in those who never completed their doctoral degrees with projections
of faculty shortages beginning in the mid 1990s (Bowen and Sosa, 1989) suggests that, at least in some respects, faculty members and graduate deans need
to alter the way in which graduate education is conducted and managed. Without addressing the question of how many Ph.D.'s American universities should
be producing, we can nonetheless insist that more than 55 percent of those
admitted into doctoral programs should receive the degree simply on the basis

My thanks to John H. D'Arms, Maresi Nerad, William C. Stebbins, Warren C. Whatley, and
Maia I. Bergman for their insightful comments on an earlier version of this chapter and to
Kay L. Paul for her patience in typing it.

of the commitment of personal and institutional resources that Ph.D. study implies. (For example, data from the University of Michigan and the University of California at Berkeley for the cohort that entered with a doctoral degree objective during the period 1978–80 show that roughly 45 percent had not completed the Ph.D. after eleven years.) Moreover, as faculty and graduate deans seek the financial resources from government, foundations, and the private sector that graduate education will need to sustain its quality over time, they are being asked to justify their completion rates.

How We Might Change the Way
We Think About Graduate Education

Let us consider a thought experiment: Suppose we wanted to change the face of doctoral education in order to reduce its frustrations. What would we do? To put it more positively, suppose that we wanted to create an environment in which 75 percent of the students admitted earned the Ph.D. in four to six years, depending on the field, with a minimum of stress (other than the stress of intellectual pursuits). Which aspects of doctoral education would we change? This chapter uses the cumulative experience of the author and other graduate deans to highlight seven aspects of the way in which doctoral education is currently managed that would have to be altered. Then it describes the policies that are necessary for producing these alterations and suggests some implications of these policies for academic departments and graduate schools.

Admissions Process. The first element in this thought experiment is that departments would have to be even more careful than they already are when selecting students for admission. They would have to try harder to identify certain personal characteristics that are germane to success: How motivated is the student to pursue graduate study? Can the student sustain the research mode of the discipline, which in some disciplines involves independent and lonely study over long periods of time? Can the student deal with ambiguity? Does the student have a sense of balance in his or her life? Does the student have realistic expectations about the nature of graduate study? Will the student be comfortable with the demands of academic life? While letters of recommendation are intended to address some of these issues, they do so imperfectly. Applicants under serious consideration for admission to doctoral study might be interviewed to add another dimension to the assessment. These interviews might prove to be far less expensive in the long run than supporting students for several years only to have them drop out. To be most effective, these interviews would have to involve not only faculty but also graduate students, since the latter might have a different and sometimes more realistic idea of the characteristics that are necessary to succeed in the program.

Graduate Curriculum. As one faculty member has suggested, the reason why students do not move through their programs expeditiously and complete them in greater numbers is not that they do not try to progress but that there is too much for them to have to get through. This observation suggests that, in our thought experiment, departments would have to engage in frequent reconsiderations of their doctoral program. They would want to be sure both that the requirements were still germane to the field (or fields, in the case of interdisciplinary programs) and that the requirements could be met in a timely fashion. Have new requirements been added and older ones not dropped? The process of accretion is bound to increase time to degree. And department chairs would have to examine patterns of faculty sabbatical and other leaves to see whether they allowed students to satisfy course requirements in a reasonable amount of time. At one research university, a faculty member in a key departmental subspeciality was granted a two-year leave with no provision for a substitute. His students were unable to take required courses until he returned, a situation that one student characterized as graduate school limbo.

A related issue affecting both students' time to degree and retention concerns the transitions between course work and preliminary examinations, preliminary examinations and the prospectus, and the prospectus and the dissertation. Departments or programs in the humanities and the more humanistically oriented social sciences sometimes view each of these as a separate milestone and do not indicate to students that one stage of doctoral work leads to the next. Students in these programs take longer to complete their degrees than do students in the sciences, where dissertation projects may begin as early as the second year. (For example, comparative data by program gathered by graduate schools at the University of California at Berkeley and the University of Michigan for the period between 1980 and 1987 indicate that the mean for graduate students in the sciences to complete a doctorate was 6.2 years, while the mean for students in the humanities was 8.2 years.)

The collaborative nature of work in laboratory science is a distinctive feature of that culture, and it cannot easily be reproduced in the humanities and the more humanistically oriented social sciences, where scholarship is most often undertaken alone. Nonetheless, creating research seminars in the humanities that would require the student to present independent work in the third year of the program would help the student begin to seek out dissertation topics. Replacing or augmenting preliminary examinations with courses geared to introduce students to bibliographical and other techniques involved in the dissertation would have to be considered, so students would not flounder before identifying a dissertation topic and writing a prospectus.

Expectations about the nature and scope of the dissertation itself would have to be reexamined in certain fields, although such a reexamination is very difficult, since expectations in this area are usually established by the national (or international) norms of the discipline, not by the department.

Advising and Mentoring Graduate Students. To improve the success rate of doctoral education, work with graduate students would have to have the importance now accorded to other aspects of a faculty member's performance, namely, research and undergraduate teaching. The teaching, advising, and mentoring of graduate students are not always distinct processes, but they are separable aspects of graduate education. In the early stages of students' careers, *advising* means offering academic information and counsel. In the later stages, it means serving on students' doctoral committees. To measure excellence in advising, faculty members would have to report on the status of their graduate students at regular intervals—at least annually. Anonymous evaluations of advising by graduate students (perhaps also by alumni) would have to be considered in promotion and tenure decisions, much as teaching performance already is. Faculty who prove to be unsuccessful at advising graduate students would have to be given increased teaching or other assignments.

Mentoring graduate students goes beyond merely advising them. *Mentorship* means behaving in ways that indicate respect for students as sources of ideas and insights (coauthoring papers with them is one way of demonstrating this respect in fields where jointly authored papers are appropriate), offering students timely and constructive responses to their work (for example, by returning dissertation chapters within weeks rather than months), modeling the values of the discipline for them, and demonstrating a concern for their professional welfare (for example, by helping them to obtain academic positions). In short, mentorship means coming to treat students as colleagues, not as apprentices.

Although individuals at nearly all stages of life can benefit from mentorship, graduate students may be especially in need of it. As the sociologist Morris Zelditch, Jr., (1990) stated in a speech to graduate deans at Arizona State University, mentorship is essential to graduate education for three reasons. First, graduate education, at least in some respects, is job training, and it can be enhanced by having a mentor who is well placed in networks that can benefit the student. Second, because mentoring focuses on methods and means of creating knowledge, it is best done by someone who is experienced in the creation of knowledge. Third, mentoring involves socialization to the values, norms, practices, procedures, and attitudes of the discipline and the academy, and such learning is best transmitted by someone who is already a member of the profession.

One might add a fourth reason to this short list: Writing a dissertation involves a set of risks, precisely because the objective is to create knowledge, not merely to record what is already known. The mentor, who has far greater experience in the discipline, can help the student to assess the risks inherent in a given research direction and indicate what constitutes a manageable task with a productive outcome. In other words, having a mentor would be essential to graduate education because the mentor can help (but not guarantee) that writing the dissertation does not become a Sisyphean task. Although it is possible for students to work on their own (many good ones do), students should ideally be able to count on the help of one or more faculty mentors who take an interest in their work, guide them through it expeditiously, and model the values and aspirations of the profession for them. As Chapter Three in this volume suggests, providing adequate mentorship to graduate students would help to improve the success rate in doctoral work.

Tracking Graduate Students' Progress. Keeping track of students' progress at every stage of the graduate career is almost as important as admitting students who are well suited to graduate study. Tracking students adequately means far more than merely assigning an adviser and giving them a list of departmental regulations. It means making sure that the relationship between adviser and advisee is comfortable for both, and it means checking with the student at regular intervals during every stage of graduate school—course work, preliminary examinations, prospectus writing, dissertation writing, and the oral defense—to be sure that the student's expectations and accomplishments are both what they should be. In fact, requiring faculty to make at least annual reports of progress both to the department and to the student could be vitally important in reducing attrition in graduate programs: Students who do not receive such reports may have no veridical idea of their progress in a program, since the narrow grading scale that graduate faculty generally use may give students in academic difficulty a false sense of well-being and no indication of how to improve.

Mechanisms for Financial Support. It is generally accepted that adequate financial support is central to the pace of students' graduate education. Yet some students make reasonable progress while teaching term after term, while others with full fellowship support languish. The picture is, thus, more complicated than one might at first suppose: Teaching responsibilities may help to strengthen a student's commitment to the field, while research assistantships that require extensive work on a faculty member's project may slow a student's own research. It is now clear that it is the mix and timing of support, not the mere presence of support, that is critical, together with an appropriately supportive environment (Bowen and Rudenstine, 1992).

To assist in this process, graduate schools would have to examine the types and mixtures of support that they offered and consider targeting aid to the moments in a graduate student's career when it would make the most difference (first-year fellowships in the sciences, dissertation fellowships in the humanities and the more humanistically oriented social sciences). Graduate schools would also have to analyze the effectiveness of other institutional forms of support. For example, students sometimes find that research assistantships are exploitative and leave them with few opportunities to pursue their own work. Although virtually no graduate school believes that its support of doctoral students is adequate, few would not benefit from a reexamination of the mechanisms and timing that makes this support available to students.

Climate for Graduate Education. Students sometimes report that the climate for graduate education in their department inhibits their efforts. By this they mean that faculty seem to be hostile or intimidating or that faculty treat them capriciously. Other students encounter racial or sexual harassment or find that they are evaluated not for their intellectual capacities but on the basis of extraneous factors over which they have no control. Problems of this sort can linger in a student's consciousness, coloring views of the graduate experience and hampering success. To increase Ph.D. completion rates and students' satisfaction with their graduate experience, graduate schools and academic departments would have to examine these aspects of the environment more carefully in order to make the treatment of students less discriminatory and more humane.

Practices and Procedures. As the last part of this thought experiment, graduate schools and faculty would have to look anew at the practices and procedures governing graduate education with an eye to making them as simple, helpful, and effective as possible. This process would require frequent reviews with the focus always on the students' welfare. Two questions—Why do we do things this way? and Could we change our practices and procedures to reduce work for the department, the graduate school, or the student?—would be healthy starting points for this enterprise.

Any serious reconsideration of graduate study aimed at enhancing student success and satisfaction would need to take these seven factors into account. However, before we consider the ways of addressing them, we need to examine the complex context within which policies for graduate education are set.

Context for Policies That Govern Graduate Education

The work of graduate education takes place in departments and programs between faculty and students, but the policy locus is often divided between the department or program and the graduate school, with the graduate school having overall responsibility for the quality and pace of graduate education.

Moreover, graduate deans watch national trends and projections and endeavor to shape policies in accordance with national needs. Over the last few years, such organizations as the Association for Graduate Schools in the Association of American Universities (AGS/AAU) and the Council of Graduate Schools (CGS) have issued policy directives (Association of American Universities, 1990; Council of Graduate Schools, 1991). These directives were at least in part a response to the seminal volume by Bowen and Sosa (1989). Its authors argued that, if demographic projections about undergraduate curricular requirements and faculty retirement patterns held, the United States would face faculty shortages of significant proportions by 1997 in all fields, especially in the humanities and the social sciences. This argument, coupled with evidence that time to degree had lengthened and attrition in doctoral programs had increased, led the authors to recommend that graduate schools and faculty reexamine the process of graduate education to see how these factors might be altered. Since this volume appeared, economic conditions for higher education across the country have worsened. For example, nearly 60 percent of all colleges and universities had experienced cuts in their operating budgets during 1991–92 (Nicklin, 1992). Many universities have had to cancel posted new appointments. Some have had to lay off nontenured or tenured faculty. There has also been some reassessment of the data measuring time to degree (Bowen, Lord, and Sosa, 1991), but the overall conclusions still stand: Excessively long time to degree and high attrition, especially at the postcandidacy stage, sap our society's human and financial resources. Information from a recent American Council of Education survey suggests that the trend of hiring freezes and faculty layoffs will be reversed (Nicklin, 1992). This forecast is based on the finding that more than half the colleges and universities surveyed expected faculty hiring to increase on the basis of the faculty retirements and increased undergraduate enrollments that the institutions project.

Creating New Policies for Graduate Education

For graduate schools to respond appropriately to these conditions, the policies governing graduate education must be reexamined. However, for this reexamination to be effective, its objectives must be understood and supported both by faculty and the graduate school. Policy change is a cooperative venture: Neither the departments nor the graduate school can work well in isolation. Thus, a collegial dialogue must be created, in which deans, who are perhaps better in touch with national trends, work to convince faculty of the need for policy change and faculty, who actually educate graduate students, advise graduate deans as to whether the policy changes under consideration can be realized in practice.

The process has another component: The academic cultures that characterize a university are diverse. By *academic cultures* is meant the knowledge, values, and mores that distinguish one discipline from another. As Tony Becher (1989, p. 20) puts it, "The attitudes, activities, and cognitive styles of groups of academics representing a particular discipline are closely bound up with the characteristics and structures of the knowledge domains with which such groups are professionally concerned." The implication of this argument for the policies and practices of graduate education is that the more we know about the differences in academic culture in graduate programs and the ways in which faculty and graduate students work within them, the more convincing we can be in proposing changes. For example, the norm in the field of history is that a student's dissertation will become his or her first book, and whether the individual eventually receives tenure depends largely on the quality of that book. Thus, history departments expect their students' dissertations to constitute original contributions to knowledge that take several years to complete. Contrast this with the norm in many science departments, where students take a different professional path that may include three to four years of postdoctoral experience. In some science fields, a dissertation can be assembled from articles that the student has worked on, perhaps with several others, which are augmented by an introduction, a literature survey, and a conclusion. Dissertations in science fields can be written in a year or less. Therefore, dissertations serve somewhat different functions in different fields. Understanding and working with these differences, which usually have a national rather than a local basis, is essential. Lockstep policies that do not take them into account will only create resentment, not effective change.

If increasing the success of doctoral students becomes an aspiration of graduate programs across the country, increasing retention will necessarily become a policy objective for them. The key question again becomes one of how to make this policy effective. The work of psychologist Karl Weick (1984) points in one fruitful direction. In the context of social problems generally, Weick (1984, p. 40) argues that "people often define social problems in ways that overwhelm their ability to do anything about them" and proposes "recast[ing] larger problems into smaller, less arousing problems, [so that] people can identify a series of controllable opportunities of modest size that produce visible results and that can be gathered into synoptic solutions. This strategy of small wins addresses social problems by working directly on their construction and indirectly on their resolution."

This proposal seems to be applicable to issues of success in doctoral education. While the task of improving retention and enhancing success may seem daunting, confronting the practices and procedures that define this policy at the level of the graduate school and the department may constitute a manageable series of small wins.

Changing Practices and Procedures of Graduate Education

As a way of institutionalizing the implications of the thought experiment with which this chapter began, we might consider some recent activities at the University of Michigan. Three years ago, in view of the national studies cited earlier and internal data concerning both the length of time it took students to complete their Ph.D. and the number of students entering doctoral programs—roughly 45 percent—who failed to achieve one, the graduate school decided to reexamine the ways in which it supported doctoral education. The new policy objective was twofold: to decrease time to the doctorate, especially in the social sciences and the humanities, and to increase the number of students who completed their degree.

The dean and the associate deans became advocates for this two-pronged policy at every opportunity: at annual meetings with department and program chairs, at special meetings convened for this purpose with a selected set of departments and programs, at the annual convocation for new graduate students, at meetings of the graduate student forum (made up of two representatives from each department and program), during periodic visits to graduate programs that served as mini reviews of these programs, and at every ad hoc session with graduate students and faculty that was convened.

Admissions Process. Improving the admissions process is one of the most challenging issues for any graduate school, since the process rests squarely in the hands of departments and the capacity to predict achievement in graduate school is so inexpert. Departments continue to assess their selection factors, which at present assume that successful undergraduate records correlate with productive graduate school careers. It might be reasonable to expect departments to assume some responsibility for helping to nourish the personal characteristics necessary for success (such as perseverance and tolerance of ambiguity) during the students' graduate careers if students do not demonstrate these attributes prior to admission. The graduate school has made some money available to departments that want to target minority and other outstanding students for recruiting visits to campus.

Graduate Curriculum. There is some evidence that the beliefs of faculty about the amount of time that should be spent on a dissertation have changed. For example, in response to a Council of Graduate Schools (1991) survey on the dissertation in 1990, faculty at the University of Michigan agreed that time spent on the dissertation should be shortened, although opinions on the feasibility of a two- or three-year timetable were varied. That was in sharp contrast to the 1976 University of Michigan study, which found that only 12 percent of the faculty surveyed felt it would be desirable to shorten the dissertation phase (Horace H. Rackham School of Graduate Studies, 1976). It is anticipated that departments will take the function of the dissertation in their discipline into account and continue to reevaluate the nature and scope of the dissertation over time.

Advising and Mentoring Graduate Students and Tracking Graduate Students' Progress. In an effort to deal constructively rather than punitively with the new emphasis on time to degree and attrition, the graduate school has focused attention on principles of good advising by issuing a small booklet outlining these ideas (Horace H. Rackham School of Graduate Studies, 1992). The booklet concentrates on what a graduate student should look for in selecting a major adviser, enlisting departmental members of the doctoral committee, and choosing the cognate member of the doctoral committee whose discipline lies outside the graduate student's primary field. On the premise that no one really trains faculty, especially junior faculty, for this task, the booklet contains sections addressing the advisers themselves. These sections outline the adviser's responsibilities and what he or she should expect of the student. Demand for the booklet has far exceeded expectations.

Mechanisms for Financial Support. Two new fellowship programs were created and made available at the postcandidacy and dissertation-writing stages to a few programs in the humanities and the humanistically oriented social sciences. These fellowships were supported in part by internal funds and in part by funds secured from a foundation. In order to select the departments that would be eligible for the new fellowships, a careful examination of progress toward decreasing time to degree and attrition was begun.

This process captured the attention of a number of departments, and some changes were evident almost immediately in the way faculty and graduate students went about the enterprise of graduate education. After a little more than a year, they reported that bringing time to degree considerations to the attention of graduate students and faculty had had a considerable hortatory effect. That factor alone seemed to have influenced the pace of many students' progress. Graduate students were being involved in discussions of the nature of their programs and what could be done to improve them. Curriculum was being changed. Preliminary examinations were scheduled earlier and better organized. Course work requirements had been streamlined. Research seminars had been created. Distribution requirements and thesis-orienting seminars had replaced preliminary examinations, and candidacy had been redefined to include the writing of a prospectus. Some departments were considering requests for faculty leaves to be incomplete unless they included a discussion of how advanced graduate students would be assisted in the faculty member's absence. Mentorship issues were being addressed to ensure that doctoral students would receive adequate attention at all stages of their work. Some departments had reduced the number of entering students that they accepted in an attempt to support and mentor their students more adequately. Other departments were "counseling out" students who could not succeed academically as soon as these students were recognized. Finally, in conjunction with efforts to decrease the number of its graduate students, one humanities department eliminated its master's program and revised the structure of its financial support of doctoral students so that all students could be fully supported through their careers without having to rely excessively on teaching assistantships.

Climate for Graduate Education. With regard to the climate for graduate education, the dean and the associate deans have tried to be especially sensitive to charges of racism and sexism by paying a visit to departments in which these concerns have been raised. They have tied some of the discretionary fellowship support that is given to troubled departments to progress in addressing these issues. The departments in which the climate for all graduate students is not what it should be have proved even more difficult to work with. In these departments, humiliation seems to characterize encounters with faculty for too many graduate students. While institutional policies are clear that such behavior is unacceptable, effecting lasting behavioral change continues to present a challenge. The dean and the associate deans are not sanguine about speedy improvement because the academic culture of certain disciplines seems to support such behavior, but they will continue to try to eradicate it.

In other departments, the climate is supportive of nearly all graduate students. These departments offer regularly scheduled intellectual and social activities that bring faculty and students together. Any hint of faculty or student racism or sexism is faced squarely, and departmental workshops are held around these issues. Graduate schools may want to encourage the sharing of successful strategies to combat racism and sexism across departments as a way of encouraging thoughtful exchange about them.

Practices and Procedures. The graduate school has also looked intensively at those of its practices and procedures that bear directly on graduate students. It has ceased intervening in a number of areas (for example, in the processing of applications for incomplete grades in courses), and it has made improvements in the way graduate students are treated (for example, by reducing the time and import of the dissertation format check). This process will be continued until the bureaucratic apparatus is reduced to a minimum.

Conclusion

Inevitably, factors beyond our control in the lives of graduate students will bear in significant ways on whether and how quickly they complete their programs. These factors include economic considerations (many graduate students will need to work full-time in order to support themselves, and the task will prove too difficult to allow them to continue in school); personal or family illness; responsibilities for children or parents that cannot be delegated to others; and spousal or significant other considerations that lead the individual to move to another setting. Some students will transfer to other graduate schools and complete their degrees there, an outcome that, given the present state of data collection among graduate schools in the United States, is impossible to track. Nevertheless, institutions can control many of the factors that influence time to degree and attrition, and here there is much that can be done. For example, preliminary data at the University of Michigan show that, for the cohorts of 1975–75, 1978–80, and 1981–83, international students completed their degrees more quickly than did domestic students and that, while women (with the exception of those in the biological and health sciences) were more likely to take longer to complete their degrees, the pace of their work was faster in departments where women were present in significant numbers. These findings suggest that study of these two groups would be fruitful.

Thus, while some attrition in graduate programs is inevitable—not everyone who aspires to a doctoral degree and is admitted to a graduate program will achieve one—it is in the interest of the student, the institution, and society as a whole for the percentage of students completing their doctoral degree to increase. And while the intellectual vitality of graduate education has never been in question, there is still much that graduate deans and faculty can do to improve the level of satisfaction with graduate programs. Chief among them is making their students' graduate experience less alienating. If they succeed in this, they will have helped to dissipate the more unpleasant aspects of the reputation that graduate schools have with those who left them—with or without degrees—and with society as a whole.

References

Association of American Universities. *Institutional Policies to Improve Doctoral Education.* Washington, D.C.: Association of American Universities and Association of Graduate Schools, 1990.

Beach, T. A. "Beautiful Writing." Tulsa, Okla.: McFarlin Library at the University of Tulsa. Cited in *Chronicle of Higher Education*, Aug. 5, 1992, p. B36.

Becher, T. *Academic Tribes and Territories: Intellectual Enquiry and the Cultures of Disciplines.* Bristol, Pa.: Society for Research into Higher Education and Open University Press, 1989.

Bowen, W. G., Lord, G., and Sosa, J. A. "Measuring Time to the Doctorate: Reinterpretation of the Evidence." *Proceedings of the National Academy of Sciences,* 1991, *88,* 713–717.

Bowen, W. G., and Rudenstine, N. L. *In Pursuit of the Ph.D.* Princeton, N.J.: Princeton University Press, 1992.

Bowen, W. G., and Sosa, J. A. *Prospects for Faculty in the Arts and Sciences.* Princeton, N.J.: Princeton University Press, 1989.

Council of Graduate Schools. *The Role and Nature of the Doctoral Dissertation.* Washington, D.C.: Council of Graduate Schools, 1991.

Horace H. Rackham School of Graduate Studies. "Summary of the Report of the Dissertation Review Committee." Horace H. Rackham School of Graduate Studies, University of Michigan, 1976.

Horace H. Rackham School of Graduate Studies. *Enhancing the Academic Environment for Doctoral Students.* Ann Arbor: Horace H. Rackham School of Graduate Studies, University of Michigan, 1992.

Nicklin, J. L. "60% of All Colleges Hit by Cuts in Operating Budgets, Survey Shows." *Chronicle of Higher Education,* Aug. 5, 1992, p. A25.

Weick, K. E. "Small Wins: Refining the Scale of Social Problems." *American Psychologist,* 1984, *39* (1), 40–49.

Zelditch, M. "Mentor Roles." Paper presented at Meetings of the Western Association of Graduate Schools, Mar. 1990, Tempe, Ariz.

SUSAN S. LIPSCHUTZ is senior associate dean of the Horace H. Rackham School of Graduate Studies at the University of Michigan and teaches in the university's philosophy department.

Key resources for understanding, researching, and increasing graduate student retention and degree attainment are identified.

Studying Graduate Student Retention and Degree Attainment: Resources for Researchers

Leonard L. Baird

This chapter identifies key resources for understanding and conducting studies of graduate students and their educational experiences. Some of these resources have been available for some time, but a number reflect the growing recognition of the importance of graduate education. As Bowen and Rudenstine (1992, p. xv) put it, graduate education "occupies a particularly critical place in the overall structure of higher education because it is the training ground for almost all those who become faculty members as well as for many who pursue other vocations of broad import."

These resources on what Derek Bok (cited in Bowen and Rudenstine, 1992, p. xv) has called "the soft underbelly of the research university" are intended to provide some perspectives on a form of education that we tend to assume we know all about. In fact, although graduate education enjoys enormous prestige, it is relatively unexamined and not carefully monitored. Thus, some fairly elementary information about graduate education is often missing. The resources identified in this chapter provide guidelines for obtaining needed information and procedures for conducting evaluations and research in graduate education.

This chapter has four sections. The first reviews resources that describe the history of graduate education, its current forms, and the areas of dispute, which all increase understanding of graduate education. The second section describes methodologies, strategies and techniques that can be used in conducting research studies. The third section includes resources on particular policy issues, such as minority student progress, that might be especially important on particular campuses. The fourth section lists organizations concerned with graduate education that can be contacted for publications and advice.

General Perspectives

Baird, L. L. "The Melancholy of Anatomy: The Personal and Professional Development of Graduate and Professional School Students." In J. C. Smart (ed.), *Higher Education: Handbook of Theory and Research*. Vol. 6. New York: Agathon Press, 1990.

Baird describes the dominant models of graduate and professional school education, which are based on elite institutions and prestigious fields of study. The results of various studies of the graduate school experience are reviewed and contrasted with the experience of students in professional schools. The main differences lie in the greater clarity, structure, and specificity of professional education and in the greater flexibility, openness, and creativity of graduate education. Each emphasis leads to forms of stress for students. However, most of the research on which these analyses are based has been conducted in a select group of universities and fields that do not include the majority of graduate and professional students. This majority pursues pragmatic career-oriented fields, usually master's programs, often part-time and often after or simultaneously with full-time employment. Recommendations for research on these students as well as other topics end the chapter.

Berelson, B. *Graduate Education in the United States*. New York: McGraw-Hill, 1960.

Although decades old, Berelson's comprehensive treatment of graduate education is remarkably current and valuable. It remains the only full treatment of the area in print. The topics and disputes have changed little, and Berelson's analyses are still fresh and insightful. He begins by describing the development of graduate education—how the collegiate and university models were combined to arrive at the form now prevailing in our institutions, how the form was professionalized, how professionalization has grown and research has come to dominate. Berelson discusses and presents data on the duration of doctoral study; attrition; the meaning and length of the dissertation; the role and status of master's degrees; postdoctoral work; language, qualifying, and final defense examinations; and the evaluation of programs. He also discusses a variety of proposed changes in policies and practice. Throughout these discussions, Berelson gives examples of data that can provide suggestions for today's institutional researchers examining graduate education as well as discussions that remain helpful and cogent—often more helpful and cogent than what one finds in contemporary literature.

Bowen, W. G., and Rudenstine, N. L. *In Pursuit of the Ph.D.* Princeton, N.J.: Princeton University Press, 1992.

Bowen and Rudenstine are concerned primarily with the factors influencing completion rates and only secondarily with time to degree. Using data from ten prestigious universities, National Research Council files, and national fellowship programs, the authors consider a wide variety of issues in graduate education. Besides the usual field differences (humanities with low completion rates and high times to degree and physical sciences with high completion rates and low times to degree), the authors also report that smaller departments had higher completion rates and shorter times to the doctorate; that students who had to rely on their own financial resources dropped out more often and took longer to complete the degree than students with support from university or national fellowships; that students with teaching assistantships may participate more in department life than students with fellowships and therefore more often complete their studies; and that there is a gender gap, with women dropping out more often and taking longer to complete than men. The authors examine the internal operations of departments in detail and offer a set of recommendations about financial aid funding policies, clarity of expectations, timing of requirements, monitoring of dissertation progress, mechanisms for ensuring progress on the dissertation, faculty advising, and reporting data on progress. Their discussions of these issues are illuminating and sometimes humorous.

Conrad, C. F., Haworth, J. G., and Millar, S. B. *A Silent Success: Master's Education in the United States*. Baltimore, Md.: Johns Hopkins University Press, 1993.
    These authors examine the largest but most neglected segment of graduate study, master's education. In contrast to the low regard in which some administrators and faculty hold it, the authors consider the master's degree the silent success of the title. After developing a typology of master's programs, they report on their interviews with nearly eight hundred people. These students, alumni, faculty, and employers place great value on master's education and see it as leading to such positive outcomes as analytical skills, a sense of perspective, the ability to connect theory and practice, and improved communication and professional skills. Finally, the authors profile high-quality programs and provide specific recommendations for improving master's education. The book is a valuable contribution to understanding this often ignored but very important part of graduate education.

Malaney, G. D. "Graduate Education as an Area of Research in the Field of Higher Education." In J. C. Smart (ed.), *Higher Education: Handbook of Theory and Research*. Vol. 6. New York: Agathon Press, 1988.
    This useful chapter summarizes the literature on graduate education published since 1976. The areas most often studied were matriculation issues, prediction of student performance, and gender issues, although the author identifies and reviews fifteen other areas. Most studies were conducted within single institutions, and most did not differentiate between master's- and doctoral-level work. After reviewing the content of these studies, Malaney recommends some areas for further research, including noncognitive predictors of

performance, finances, theories of graduate student development, minorities, the effects of rules and regulations, organizational structure, and decision making and power in graduate education.

Pelczar, M. J., and Solmon, L. C. (eds.). *Keeping Graduate Programs Responsive to National Needs.* New Directions for Higher Education, no. 46. San Francisco: Jossey-Bass, 1984.

The sixteen relatively brief chapters in this volume describe the past performance of graduate education and analyze the need for changes. The authors discuss prospects for and impediments to innovations in a variety of areas of graduate education, such as education and engineering, and in particular issues, such as university-industry partnerships. Albrecht's chapter on the impediments to innovation and Bowen's chapter on the social responsibility of graduate education are particularly valuable.

Pelikan, J. *Scholarship and Its Survival: Questions on the Idea of Graduate Education.* New York: Carnegie Foundation for the Advancement of Teaching, 1983.

Pelikan calls for standards for graduate students, particularly to promote integrity. He also advocates programs that make connections—not only through interdisciplinary work but also through collaboration among undergraduate, graduate, and professional schools. For true scholarship to survive, according to Pelikan, we must overcome the provincialism inherent in our disciplines while strengthening our attention to principles.

Solow, R. M. "Discussion: Educating and Training New Economics Ph.D.'s: How Good a Job Are We Doing?" *American Economic Review,* 1990, *80* (2), 437–450.

Solow discusses the results of a survey of the views of recent Ph.D.'s in economics on the quality of their graduate education and examines details of curricula, advising, dissertation requirements, and so forth. Solow's article provides a good example of the discipline-specific surveys of graduate education that can be adapted at the institutional level. It also shows how some issues in graduate student progress need to be considered within disciplines, while others can be viewed across disciplines. The article is worth reading for its thoughtful discussion by a Nobel Prize winner.

Ziolkowski, T. "The Ph.D. Squid." *American Scholar,* 1990, *59* (2), 177–195.

Ziolkowski's essay is a fine, brief general introduction to the state of doctoral education today. He discusses the historical and current narrow meaning of the Ph.D. and how it merely represents the ability to do research in some specific area. He also discusses the shift away from arts and humanities, ABDs (students who have completed all requirements except their dissertations, hence "All But Dissertations"), changes in disciplinary expectations, the meaning of the dissertation, and the lengthening of time to the degree.

Methodologies

Gillingham, L., Seneca, J. J., and Taussig, M. K. "The Determinants of Progress to the Doctoral Degree." *Research in Higher Education,* 1991, *32,* 449–468.

The authors of this study, which was conducted at Rutgers University, show how time to degree can be examined by asking current students to indicate the amount of time that they will need to obtain their degree. This estimate is then added to the time that individual students have already spent pursuing the degree to yield a total projected time to degree for each student that can then be averaged over all students or by separate departments. Thus, this study shows how cross-sectional data can be used to study the duration of graduate study. The authors were also interested in the economics of time to degree. Using least-squares regression, they found that humanities students and students who work relatively many hours expected to take longer than other students to obtain their degrees. The authors also found that family income was related negatively to time to degree among U.S. citizens and positively among foreign students. Other comparisons of U.S. and foreign students lead the authors to reflect on the different situations of the two groups.

Girves, J. E., and Wemmerus, V. "Developing Models of Graduate Student Progress." *Journal of Higher Education,* 1988, *59,* 163–189.

Girves and Wemmerus show how one institution conducted a study of student degree progress by combining official records with the results of a survey of students' experiences. The study used hierarchical regression analysis to predict progress toward degree attainment at the master's and doctoral levels. Graduate grades predicted degree progress at the master's level and involvement with one's program at the doctoral level. Students' relationships with faculty and departmental characteristics were important at both levels. The authors recommend research on three additional areas: the applicability of the models by gender, ethnicity, and foreign or domestic status; the effects of different forms of financial support; and the specific aspects of faculty-student relationships that promote progress.

Ott, M. D., Markewich, T. S., and Ochsner, N. L. "Logit Analysis of Graduate Student Retention." *Research in Higher Education,* 1984, *21,* 439–450.

This study shows how logit analysis was used at the University of Maryland to examine retention. The authors argue that logit analysis is more appropriate than multiple regression or discriminant analysis when the independent variables are categorical and the dependent variable is dichotomous, as they are in studies of retention and attrition. Substantively, they found that retention among master's students was higher among full-time and foreign students than among part-time and domestic students. Among doctoral students, retention was higher among full-time students than part-time students, and it was higher among students in some disciplines than in others.

Zwick, R. *An Analysis of Graduate School Careers in Three Universities: Differences in Attainment Patterns Across Academic Programs and Demographic Groups.* GRE Board Report No. 86-21P. Princeton, N.J.: Educational Testing Service, 1991.

Zwick shows how survival analysis, a method to chart the probability of not attaining a certain criterion over time—in this case candidacy and attainment of the doctoral degree—can be used to study student progress. Willet and Singer (1991) provide further information about the survival analysis method. Using data from three universities, Zwick calculated the patterns for eleven disciplines. The patterns for students of different ethnicity, gender, and domestic or foreign status were also charted. Candidacy and graduation rates over the first eight years after matriculation were higher in quantitatively oriented departments than they were in the humanities and social sciences. Minorities and women had lower rates, while foreign students had higher rates. Undergraduate grades and Graduate Record Examination scores were at best minimally related to candidacy and graduation within any group. The advantage of this method is that one can chart student progress and visually compare the timing of progress of students with different characteristics and academic experiences.

Specific Policy Issues

Jones, J. M., Goertz, M. E., and Kuh, C. V. (eds.). *Minorities in Graduate Education: Pipeline, Policy, and Practice.* Princeton, N.J.: Educational Testing Service, 1992.

This volume is the proceedings of a recent conference on graduate education sponsored by the Graduate Record Examinations Board. The twenty-nine contributors present discussions of statistics and original research on enrollment, degree programs, and degree attainment among minority graduate students as well as the implications of their results for policy. The focus is on the educational pipeline for minority students and on the ways in which financial aid and specific institutional practices affect their progress. Directions for future research are also discussed. This volume is useful partly because the contributors do not agree. For example, Michael Olivas criticizes much of the research on minority students for inappropriate metaphors, inadequate and misleading statistics, inappropriate aggregation of data, and ignorance of a great deal of the useful research and thinking from minority scholars. The references in each section are also useful.

Nettles, M. T. "Success in Doctoral Programs: Experiences of Minority and White Students." *American Journal of Education,* 1990, *98,* 494–522.

Nettles compared the experiences of African American and Hispanic doctoral students with those of white students at four universities and in five fields. White students had substantially higher socioeconomic status, but African Americans and Hispanics were more likely to receive fellowships and loans. African American students less often received research or teaching assistantships. Compared to other students, Hispanic students most often received assistantships, attended full-time, spent more time studying, and were most socially involved. Compared to whites, African American and Hispanic students received lower grades in graduate school and perceived greater racial discrimination, but they were also more satisfied with their doctoral programs. African American students also reported more support from their mentors than other students.

Tuckman, H., Coyle, S., and Bae, Y. *On Time to the Doctorate: A Study of the Increased Time to Complete Doctorates in Science and Engineering.* Washington, D.C.: National Academy Press, 1990.

Using the NRC files described in Chapter Five of this volume, the authors analyzed changes in time to the doctorate in eleven scientific and engineering fields between 1967 and 1986. Analysis shows that time to doctorate increased in all fields, chiefly because of increases in registered time to degree and secondarily because of interruptions in studies. Two methods were used to estimate the influence of the variables on the time measures: a common variables model used across fields and a unique variables model that allowed variables to change by field. The focus of the analysis was the change in time measures, so the basic data were the mean time measures for each year for each discipline. Increases in total time to degree were best explained by the age of students at time of entry to graduate school and in some fields by the salaries earned by doctorates who had been in the field ten years as compared with the salaries earned by recent recipients of the doctorate. No one variable was consistently related to increases in registered time to degree in all fields, although age at entry was related in several fields.

Different forms of financial support had different effects in different fields. For example, research assistantships reduced time to degree in mathematics and increased it in the biological sciences. The authors note that their unit of analysis, year by field, is only one way of examining the issue. They recommend the kind of individual analysis described by Ploskonka in Chapter Five of this volume.

The authors end their report with a discussion of possible explanations for the increases in time to the doctorate. These explanations include the idea that the body of knowledge in most fields has increased so dramatically that students need longer to master it in a doctoral program, that the increases are due to institutional policies, that students find graduate school comfortable and do not wish to leave, that changes in financial aid policies have caused programs to lengthen, and that the job market for doctorates has become less appealing. The authors also discuss the implications of increases in time to doctorate, including higher costs per doctorate, longer periods before students can enter their fields as full professionals, increased attrition, and lower returns for graduate study.

White, P. E. *Women and Minorities in Science and Engineering: An Update.* Washington, D.C.: National Science Foundation, 1992.

Although not exclusively concerned with graduate education, this volume places the graduate education of women and minorities in a context of employment and labor market conditions, precollege preparation, and undergraduate education. The national figures for graduate enrollments, degree attainment rates, degree production, sources of support for doctoral students, and post-doctoral appointments are presented and described for women, blacks, Asians, Native Americans, and Hispanics. The same data for persons with physical disabilities are also presented and described. This volume provides a great deal of information that institutions that wish to study the graduate careers of the groups just mentioned will find useful.

Willie, C. V., Grady, M. K., and Hope, R. O. *African Americans and the Doctoral Experience: Implications for Policy.* New York: Teachers College Press, 1991.

This volume traces the participation of African Americans in higher education and examines the effects of financial aid policies and academic preparation on African American students. Concentrating on black colleges and the United Negro College Fund, most of the book describes a Lilly Endowment–sponsored program designed to assist faculty members at private black colleges to obtain their doctorates. The program, which was generally successful, leads the authors to a number of recommendations for increasing minority graduation rates and changes in national higher education policy.

Wimberley, D. W., McCloud, D. G., and Flinn, W. L. "Predicting Success of Indonesian Graduate Students in the United States." *Comparative Education Review,* 1992, *36,* 487–508.

International students, especially from Far Eastern countries, are increasingly common on American campuses. This study is one of the few to examine the predictors of academic performance and degree completion among international graduate students. The article shows how the predictors for at least one group, Indonesian graduate students, are very different from the predictors for U.S. citizens. For example, the presence of all the student's dependents with the student in the United States had a positive relation to both graduate grades and degree completion. The authors discuss these and other variables that may affect the success of international graduate students. Since many campuses have large numbers of international graduate students, this discussion may be widely useful.

Organizational Resources

The Council of Graduate Schools is the national organization of graduate schools. Deans or associate deans of graduate schools usually represent their institution. Although its membership is restricted, the council publishes the *Communicator,* a useful magazine/newsletter that discusses recent issues and trends in the structure and financing of graduate education. The council also publishes an annual survey of graduate enrollments and degrees, which breaks this information down by institution, discipline, gender, ethnicity, full-time or part-time status, and first-time enrollments. The council also has an office that answers queries about a wide variety of concerns in graduate education. Contact Peter D. Syverson, Council of Graduate Schools, One Dupont Circle N.W., Suite 430, Washington, D.C. 20036-1173, 202/223-3791.

The Graduate Record Examinations Board (GREB) sponsors the Graduate Record Examination (GRE) general tests as well as specific field tests, such as those in economics and physics. Since students complete a brief form when they register for the tests, personal and educational background data are available for candidates. GREB will prepare a summary report and tape for individual institutions on all students who asked that a copy of their scores be sent to the institution. An institution can use this tape as a base for its own records once it has merged the information on the tape with its own files. If an institution chooses to participate, GREB has provided a validity service that allows the institution to relate the grades that its students obtain to GRE admissions data. This service has been temporarily suspended for a year.

GREB also provides a service that allows institutions and individual programs to evaluate themselves and compare their local responses with those of other institutions. The survey, the Graduate Program Self-Assessment, has two forms. One form is designed mainly for doctoral-level education, and the other is for master's programs. Data are obtained from current students, faculty, and—if the department chooses—graduates. There is a charge for these services. The GREB also holds admissions workshops at various locations across the country. Finally, the GREB sponsors a wide range of research projects concerned with graduate education. These projects are conducted by Educational Testing Service. Contact Graduate Record Examinations Program, Educational Testing Service, Princeton, N.J. 08541-6000.

The National Research Council (NRC) prepares and scores the Survey of Earned Doctorates described by Ploskonka in Chapter Five. The NRC will prepare a tape at no charge for any institution providing survey results for the time span desired. The NRC provides documentation for the tapes. It also issues annual reports on the results from previous years disaggregated by broad fields, which may help in interpreting the results. Contact the Office of Scientific and Engineering Personnel, National Research Council, 2101 Constitution Avenue, Washington, D.C., 20418.

The National Science Foundation (NSF), in its several divisions—especially the Science Resources Studies Division—prepares numerous reports on conditions and policies in graduate education in the sciences and engineering. NSF reports usually include numerous charts and graphs illustrating such information as changes in sources of support, percentages of foreign students, and minority enrollments. This information can be compared with results for local institutions, which can help to put local findings into national and even international perspective. Contact the National Science Foundation, Washington, D.C. 20550. Information on documents can be obtained electronically by sending a message via BITNET to "stisserv@NSF" or via Internet to "stissev@nsf.gov: Request: stis Topic:index". For direct e-mail, send a message to the same addresses, but in the message text put "Request: stis Topic: stisdirm".

Reference

Willet, J. B., and Singer, F. D. "From Whether to When: New Methods for Studying Student Dropout and Teacher Attrition." *Review of Educational Research*, 1991, *61*, 407–450.

LEONARD L. BAIRD is professor and director of the Office of Higher Education Research in the Department of Educational Policy Studies and Evaluation, University of Kentucky, Lexington.

INDEX

Abedi, J., 9, 62, 63
Academic cultures, 75
Ackerman, J., 7
Adjusted goodness of fit index (AGFI), 48
Admissions: and graduate education, 70; and retention study, 21;
Advising: and attrition/time-to-degree, 33–34; and graduate education, 71–73, 77
Allison, P. D., 63
Alwin, D. F., 49
Analysis: institutional-level, of retention, 20–21; program-level, of retention, 20; quantitative/qualitative, 27, 66; regression, 42, 63. *See also* Assessment measures
Anderson, J. C., 46
Assessment measures: analysis of variance, 42; causal modeling, 42, 48–50; institutional time-to-degree, 60–67; logistic regression, 42; model fit, 47–54; structural modeling component, 50–54. *See also* Analysis
Association for Graduate Schools, 74
Association of American Universities, 74
Attrition: defined, 15; doctoral student, 16; graduate/undergraduate student, factors, 15. *See also* Attrition/time to degree; Degree completion; Retention
Attrition/time to degree: factors, 4–5, 8–9; and model of knowing, 8; models, 5–9, 31–36; and psychological factors, 6; and quantitative/qualitative analysis/methods, 27; research approaches, 9–11; research model, 31–36; and social/academic/personal factors, 8–9; and stage theory, 7; studies, 4; University of California, Berkeley (study), 27–38. *See also* Degree completion; Time to degree

Bae, Y., 4, 60, 62, 63
Baird, L. L., 4, 5, 6, 8, 10, 11, 42, 59
Balla, J. R., 48
Beach, T. A., 69
Bean, J. P., 3, 10
Becher, T., 74
Beeler, K. J., 59

Benkin, E. M., 9, 29, 62, 63
Bennett, N., 48
Bentler, P. M., 41, 48, 49
Berelson, B., 4, 60, 66, 67
Berger, J., 60
Berkenkotter, D., 7
Blum, D. E., 59
Bode, R., 42
Bonett, D. G., 48, 49
Bowen, W. G., 4, 13, 17, 18, 59, 60, 61, 66, 67, 69, 73, 74, 81
Bragg, A. K., 5
Brazziel, W. F., 59
Byrne, B. M., 48, 49, 53, 54

Cabrera, A. F., 41, 42
Campus. See University/college
Carmines, E. G., 49
Carnegie Foundation for the Advancement of Teaching, 61
Carnegie Research I university time-to-degree study, 60–67
Causal modeling, 42, 48–50
Cerny, J., 62
Chi-square/degree of freedom ratio, 48–49
Chi-square statistic, 48–49
Clark, B., 44
Coefficient of determination, 52
Completion rates: cumulative, 18–19; minimum, 17–18, 20–21; truncated, 17–18, 20–21; University of California, Berkeley, doctoral degree, 28–29. *See also* Degree completion
Converse, J. M., 10
Council of Graduate Schools, 74, 77
Council of Graduate Schools Task Force, 14
Coyle, S., 4, 60, 62, 63
Culture, academic, 75
Cumulative completion rate (CCR), 18–19. *See also* Completion rates; Degree completion
Curriculum, 70–71, 77. *See also* Graduate education

Data: graduate education, 45; graduate student progress, 9–10; retention study, 21–25; time-to-degree, 61–62

University of California, Berkeley, graduate division study: attrition/time-to-degree model, 31–36; completion length reasons, 29–30; completion rates, 28–29; cross-university comparison, 29; and faculty, 37; and graduate assistants, 38; and graduate students, 37–38; recommendations for action, 37–38; steps, 27–28; student academic patterns, 30–31; time-to-degree rates, 28

Van Alstine, J., 48
Vaughn, J. C., 62, 66

Weick, K. E., 76
Weidman, J., 5
Weinman, J. M., 61
Wemmerus, V., 4, 16
Wheaton, B., 49
Willet, J. B., 63, 86
Wilson, K. M., 4, 62, 66

Yancey, B. D., 42

Zelditch, M., 72

ORDERING INFORMATION

NEW DIRECTIONS FOR INSTITUTIONAL RESEARCH is a series of paperback books that provides planners and administrators in all types of academic institutions with guidelines in such areas as resource coordination, information analysis, program evaluation, and institutional management. Books in the series are published quarterly in spring, summer, fall, and winter and are available for purchase by subscription as well as by single copy.

SUBSCRIPTIONS for 1993 cost $47.00 for individuals (a savings of 25 percent over single-copy prices) and $62.00 for institutions, agencies, and libraries. Please do not send institutional checks for personal subscriptions. Standing orders are accepted.

SINGLE COPIES cost $15.95 when payment accompanies order. (California, New Jersey, New York, and Washington, D.C., residents please include appropriate sales tax.) Billed orders will be charged postage and handling.

DISCOUNTS FOR QUANTITY ORDERS are available. Please write to the address below for information.

ALL ORDERS must include either the name of an individual or an official purchase order number. Please submit your order as follows:
  Subscriptions: specify series and year subscription is to begin
  Single copies: include individual title code (such as IR80)

MAIL ALL ORDERS TO:
  Jossey-Bass Publishers
  350 Sansome Street
  San Francisco, CA 94104-1342

FOR SINGLE-COPY SALES OUTSIDE OF THE UNITED STATES, CONTACT:
  Maxwell Macmillan International Publishing Group
  866 Third Avenue
  New York, NY 10022-6221

FOR SUBSCRIPTION SALES OUTSIDE OF THE UNITED STATES, CONTACT:
  any international subscription agency or Jossey-Bass directly.